Main Idea

MW01040200

Grades 5-6

by
Laurie Gilbert

Published by Instructional Fair
an imprint of
Frank Schaffer Publications®

Instructional Fair

Author: Laurie Gilbert
Editors: Sara Bierling, Kathryn Wheeler, Sharon Kirkwood
Cover Artist: Sherry Neidigh
Interior Artist: Theresa Wright

Frank Schaffer Publications®

Instructional Fair is an imprint of Frank Schaffer Publications.

Send all inquiries to:
Frank Schaffer Publications
8720 Orion Place
Columbus, Ohio 43240-2111

Main Idea—grades 5–6

ISBN: 1-56822-932-1

8 9 10 11 PAT 12 11 10 09

About the Book

Through the selections in *Main Idea*, students will have the opportunity to practice finding the main idea in various types of reading selections found both in and out of the classroom. These formats include advertisements, newspapers, letters, Internet Relay Chat, travel brochures, and more. Students are asked to respond to the readings in a variety of creative ways to demonstrate their ability to make use of their knowledge of topic, details, and main idea.

Use these selections for independent practice or whole group instruction. Or, place the activity sheets in a center and reproduce the answer key for self-checking.

Table of Contents

The Enormous, Endangered Grizzly Bear

(1) Grizzly bears stand up to three and a half feet (1.0675 m) tall at the shoulders and are from six to seven feet (1.83 to 2.135 m) long. They weigh between 325 and 850 pounds (148 and 386 kg). Their name comes from their frost-tipped dorsal hairs, and their color can vary from dark brown to nearly black to pale yellow.

(2) A grizzly bear's habitat must include plenty of space; they range up to 150 square miles (390 sq km). They prefer a subalpine climate near a body of water where they can find potential den sites. This habitat must also provide diverse and abundant food. Grizzly bears eat berries, pine nuts, grasses, herbs, and sedges, but over half their diet is meat. This comes from carrion, small rodents, and malnutritioned game, which is easy to hunt. They also like to raid garbage dumps. Grizzlies must eat enough to store up fat during hibernation.

(3) The breeding season for grizzly bears is from mid-May to mid-July. A female grizzly reaches sexual maturity at about four and a half years, and a male at three and a half years. Females only reproduce every three years, while males may mate several times during one season. Grizzlies have a six-month gestation period. Once a female becomes pregnant, she begins to eat more to store up fat for herself and her cubs. She will gain up to 400 pounds (182 kg). She begins to prepare her den between October and November.

(4) Grizzly cubs are born between January and March. They will emerge from their den with their mother anywhere from late March to early May. Cubs begin to eat solid food at six months of age when their mothers teach them to hunt and forage. Fifty percent of grizzly cubs die during their first year due to malnutrition and attack by other animals. If they survive, they will den with their mothers for two winters. Grizzly bears live about 15 years, although some have been known to live for 30.

(5) The grizzly bear population is endangered. They like the same fertile areas that farmers and ranchers like. Ranchers see them as a threat to their livestock and will often shoot them. The grizzly bear habitat is shrinking because of the expansion of residential and recreational areas. Only one percent of their original historic range exists today in the lower 48 states. Because their habitat is shrinking, their populations have become isolated and their gene pool limited.

(6) Conservationists are working to improve the situation for grizzly bears. They are trying to claim back land for habitat. They tag the bears so they can follow their movements and learn more about what they need to survive. Conservationists are trying to reintroduce grizzlies into the Northern Rockies. This will increase the gene flow with the Yellowstone bears. These activists need support from concerned citizens who care about the survival of the great grizzly bear.

Name _____

Use with page 4.

The Enormous, Endangered Grizzly Bear (cont.)

Circle the answer that best tells the main idea of each numbered paragraph. Be sure to read all answers carefully before choosing one. There may be several true answers, but only one tells the main idea.

1. The main idea is ...

   a. to give a description of the grizzly bear.

   b. to give heights of grizzly bears.

   c. to explain the name origin of the grizzly bear.

2. a. A grizzly bear's habitat must have nuts, berries, and plenty of meat.

   b. A grizzly bear's habitat must be 150 square miles (390 sq km).

   c. A grizzly bear's habitat must have plenty of space, the right kind of food, and potential den sites.

3. a. Several grizzly males can mate with a single female.

   b. Grizzly females gain weight and find a den to prepare for childbirth.

   c. Grizzly bears follow specific breeding patterns.

4. a. Grizzly bears can live to be 30 years old.

   b. A grizzly bear's survival can be uncertain, but they are capable of having a long life.

   c. Fifty percent of cubs die during their first year.

5. a. Grizzly bears are endangered because of various threats to their survival.

   b. Grizzly bears are endangered by ranchers.

   c. Grizzly bear habitats are shrinking because of increased recreation and residential areas.

6. a. Grizzly bear populations should be reintroduced to their old habitat areas.

   b. Various efforts are being made to recover the grizzly bear population.

   c. Conservationists tag grizzly bears to study them.

7. The main idea of the whole article is...

   a. about grizzly bear habitats.

   b. about grizzly bear predators.

   c. about grizzly bears and what is happening to them.

The Ultimate Backpack

Read the magazine advertisement. Then, answer the questions below.

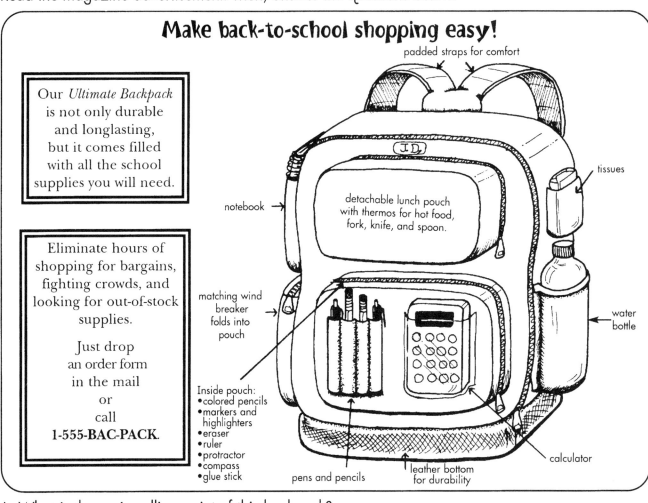

Make back-to-school shopping easy!

Our *Ultimate Backpack* is not only durable and longlasting, but it comes filled with all the school supplies you will need.

Eliminate hours of shopping for bargains, fighting crowds, and looking for out-of-stock supplies.

Just drop an order form in the mail or call **1-555-BAC-PACK**.

padded straps for comfort

notebook

detachable lunch pouch with thermos for hot food, fork, knife, and spoon.

tissues

matching wind breaker folds into pouch

Inside pouch:
•colored pencils
•markers and highlighters
•eraser
•ruler
•protractor
•compass
•glue stick

pens and pencils

water bottle

leather bottom for durability

calculator

1. What is the main selling point of this backpack?

_____

2. What are two reasons the advertisement gives to support this idea?

_____

_____

3. To whom would this advertisement appeal?

_____

4. How can you receive this product?

_____

_____

Pen Pals

Dear Jessica,

Hi, how are you? I haven't seen you for such a long time, I probably wouldn't recognize you. Did you say you got your hair cut short? Mine is still long, but it's permed now.

Guess what! The real reason I'm writing this letter is to tell you that I'm coming back to visit on the third weekend of March. My Dad has a business trip planned and he's taking me along. He said that if it's okay with your family I can stay with you instead of at the hotel with him. Please write back and let me know if that's okay. We'll come in on Thursday and leave Sunday. That way I can go to school with you on Friday to see everyone. Did anybody else move away? Is Clint still in your class? Does he have another girlfriend, or do you think he still likes me? I'm so excited, I can't wait to see you. Write back soon!

Your best friend for always,

Heather

Write a letter back to Heather, responding to the main point of her letter.

_____

_____

_____

_____

_____

_____

_____

_____

_____

_____

_____

_____

Message

You have just arrived at the home of some friends and found this note on the door with your name on it. Decode the rebus to discover the message. Then answer the question.

   friend-r-e the -don -th

the  on the  -L of

the  +lease -b+e -p and

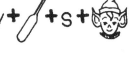 -c  T +

-c   + ies

-p the  -ep should

 by   L+8+r

What is the main idea of your friends' message? _____

_____

 Name _____

Editorials

An editorial page in a newspaper gives people an opportunity to express their opinion on an issue in a public forum. Here are two editorials, each expressing a different opinion of professional basketball players.

Dear Editor,

I think that many people in our country give too much glory to basketball players. They make millions of bucks for having fun playing a game. They get to wear expensive name-brand shoes and clothing that they don't even have to buy, and they are the ones who can afford them. They only work part of the year, and then they go on strike demanding more money. They are greedy and selfish. Sure, some of the athletes donate money to charity, but what they give is only a small fraction of what they keep for themselves. Tickets are so expensive, most kids can't afford to go to a game. Why should we continue to pay them to have fun? Basketball is just a game. Instead of worshiping someone else for playing basketball, we should be out playing ourselves.

Fed-up in Fennville

Dear Editor,

Let's hear it for the professional B-ball players! American kids need something good to believe in. Many athletes weren't always rich. Many started poor, and because of hard work, they arrived where they are today. They deserve what they have. They give all kids hope that maybe someday we could be there too. The athletes inspire us to try harder and to be the best we can, just as they are. They inspire us to get off the couch, and to play ball, have fun, and exercise. They are heroes and positive role models. We, in America, are lucky to have these athletes to look up to.

Pleased in Petoskey

Circle the correct answer.

1. Fed-up in Fennville thinks professional basketball players are...

    a. greedy and selfish.   b. giving kids hope.   c. inspiring youngsters.

2. Pleased in Petoskey thinks professional basketball players...

    a. are paid too much.

    b. donate money to charity.

    c. inspire kids and give them hope.

3. Write **F** (Fed-up in Fennville) or **P** (Pleased in Petoskey) to identify the source of each detail.

  ____ wear expensive clothing   ____ give hope   ____ demand more money

  ____ greedy and selfish   ____ exercise   ____ positive role models

  ____ get too much glory   ____ make millions   ____ weren't always rich

  ____ basketball is just a game   ____ work hard   ____ inspire

Try this: Write your own editorial expressing your opinion of professional athletes.

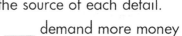

Use with page 11.

Wetlands

Wetlands are low areas that are soaked with water. They can consist of freshwater or saltwater. They can be found on the coast or inland. Wetlands include marshes, swamps, lagoons, bogs, and prairie potholes.

Wetlands are often thought of as soggy pieces of ground that are good for nothing except mosquito breeding. About a half-million acres per year are destroyed for agricultural use, malls, or housing developments. Since scientists have discovered that wetlands are a very valuable resource, many people today are trying to protect them from further destruction.

Wetlands provide shelter for many different animals including fish, birds, amphibians, reptiles, and mammals. Many of these animals could be left homeless and could face extinction without wetlands. Because the plants provide good cover, wetlands are a great breeding and nesting ground for the animals.

Migratory birds use the wetlands for a resting place as they travel back and forth between summer and winter habitats. As these birds follow the same route year after year, they depend on the wetlands that their ancestors have used for centuries. Can you imagine what would happen if they were ready to stop and rest for the night and found a mall instead of their wetland?

The plants that grow in a wetland area are an important part of the food web. They provide nutrient-rich food for all the herbivores and omnivores that live there. They, in turn, provide food for the carnivores.

Wetlands also help to prevent flooding. They provide a place for the excess water to spill out and be soaked up like a sponge. In

times of heavy rains, there is a place for the excess water to sit until it can flow out into streams.

These natural sponges also act as strainers to sift mud and other debris from the water. They trap sewage waste and allow silt to settle. The streams that flow out of wetlands are cleaner than when the water first arrives there.

Wetlands also act as a filter to clean toxins from the water. They help in the decomposition of many harmful substances. The plants in the wetlands help keep nutrient concentrations from reaching toxic levels. In some areas where wetlands have been filled, too many nitrates are entering the water, making it unsafe to drink. Because plants produce oxygen in the process of photosynthesis, plants in the wetlands also mix oxygen into the water.

Wetlands are a very valuable resource. Let's do all we can to preserve them.

Wetlands (cont.)

Each picture in the web below represents one of the attributes of the wetlands. On or next to each picture, write a phrase describing the main reason that picture represents a wetland.

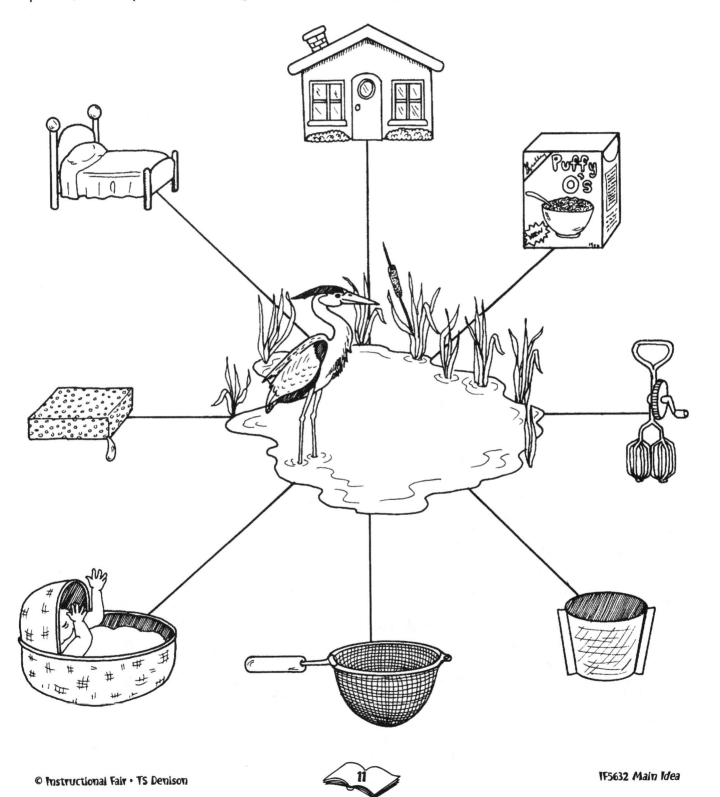

Name _____

Today's News

Hurricane Hits Hard

Hurricane Harold hit Honolulu, Hawaii, yesterday at 5:30 A.M. Tourists and residents had to evacuate hotels and homes as water levels rose to dangerous heights. Hotel Hono was hit the hardest. Windows in the lobby were broken as water gushed in, washing away chairs, tables, and hotel records. Only one of the stately palms at the entrance still stands. Fortunately, everyone was evacuated in time. There were no fatalities. Only minor injuries were reported.

Pet Problems

The town council of Pleasantville met yesterday to discuss the problems caused by pets in the city parks.

"People need to take responsibility for their pets," claimed one citizen. "The pets are running wild and producing piles of poo in the park."

"These animals present a danger to children who want to pet them. Please do something," pleaded another.

"Our animals are cooped up all day and need a place to run. The park is the only safe space," protested a pet owner.

After listening to all arguments, the mayor proposed a solution. "Anyone bringing a pet to the park must use a leash to keep it restrained. They must also carry a bag and trowel to dispose of any waste left by the pet. A one-fourth acre area of the park will be fenced off so owners can release their pets to run there without endangering the children who are playing in the park."

The proposal was unanimously approved by all those present and will go into effect next week.

Falcons Flog Pirates

The Fairview Falcons are having a fabulous football season. On Saturday, they defeated their opponents, the Pleasantville Pirates, 52–49. The Falcons' four touchdowns were scored by the flying running back Frank Fernhide. The other three were scored on fantastic passes from quarterback Fernando Fernandez to Fred Feldstone. All extra points and the final field goal were converted from the foot of Farley Fitzgerald. After the victory, the fans cheered, running onto the field

Town Pride

The Eco Club of Redville will be sponsoring a "Be Proud of Your Town" clean-up day this Saturday from 8:00–4:00. They will pick up any recyclable waste left at the curb. Please have waste separated into boxes for paper, metal, glass, and plastic. There are volunteers to help senior citizens. If you would like a volunteer to work with you, please call Angie at 555-5555 before Friday afternoon. Let's all work together to make our town "The Best Around."

Use with page 12.

Today's News (cont.)

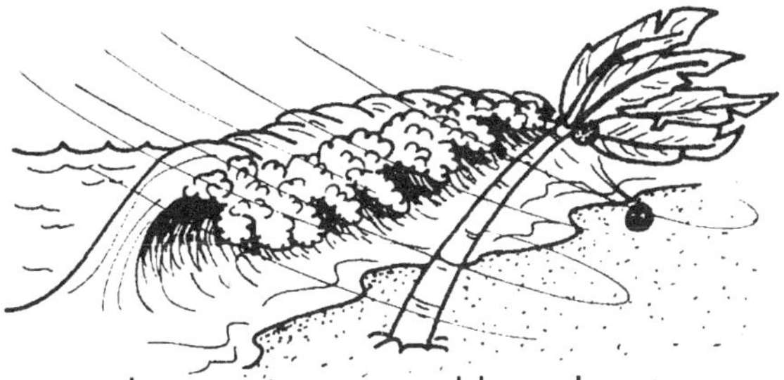

Circle the correct answer concerning these news articles.

Hurricane Hits Hard
What is the main message of this article?

a. A hurricane hit Honolulu.
b. Tourists and residents were evacuated.

c. Hotel Hono was ruined by a hurricane.
d. No fatalities ocurred.

Pet Problems
The conflict is between...

a. dogs and kids.
b. the mayor and the citizens.

c. dog owners and other citizens.
d. pets and city parks.

Complete the following.

Falcons Flog Pirates
Who won the game? _____

Who scored the most touchdowns? _____

Town Pride
On what day and at what time is the clean-up being held? _____

Where should waste be left? _____

Whom should you call for assistance? _____

Extra, Extra!

Find an article in your local newspaper. Write the main idea of the article in one or two sentences, including the who, what, when, where, and why. Give a news report to your class.

_____

_____

_____

_____

_____

_____

_____

_____

_____

Ski Bums

Listen in on this phone conversation.

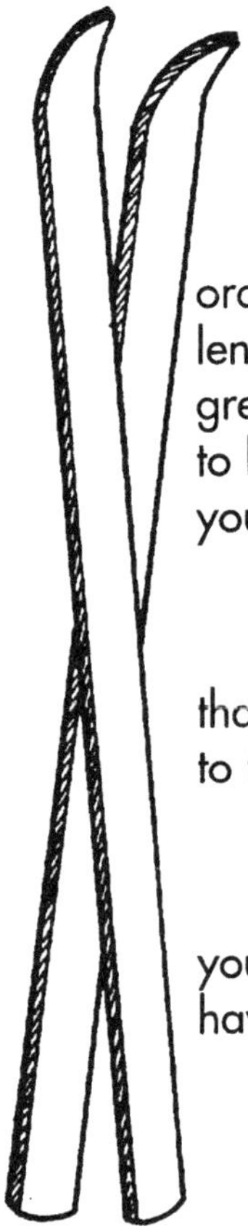

"Hello, this is the Bedford residence. Hannah speaking."

"Hi, is Bill at home?"

"He's not able to come to the phone right now. May I take a message?"

"Yes. This is Dan from Nordic Ski Sales. Please tell him we received his order for skis, poles, bindings, boots, hat, mittens, wool socks, and polypropylene shirt. I really like the hat he picked. I bought the same one myself. He got a great deal on those socks too. They normally retail for $7.98. His order is ready to be shipped, but we have one problem. He forgot to tell us his boot size. Do you happen to know what size he wears?"

"No, only that they're big."

"Well, he needs to call and tell us the size he wants. We want to be sure that he is happy with the fit. Does he have our phone number, or would he prefer to fax us?"

"Probably phone."

"Okay, the number is 1-555-SKI BUMS. That's 1-555-754-2867, in case you can't figure out the numbers. Tell him the sooner he calls, the sooner we will have him on skis!"

"Okay, thanks. Goodbye."

"Bye."

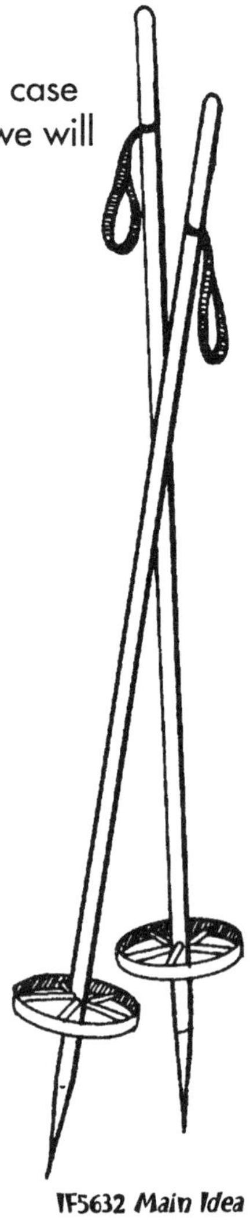

Please leave a message for Bill, telling only the main idea.

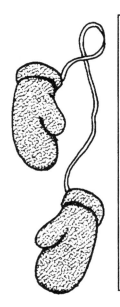

Message for: _____

From: _____

Main idea of the message: _____

_____

_____

_____

_____

_____

_____

Photocopy page 15. Cut on the solid outer lines of the brochure. Based on the information on the brochure, design a map of Natural Wonders Park on the back side of the sheet. Then, complete the middle panel. Finally, fold the paper on the dotted lines to form a two-fold brochure. First fold in line b, then line a.

Come to Natural Wonders Park

and have the experience of visiting spectacular sights from around the country all in one convenient location.

- Walk the sandy beaches of the island.
- Explore a tide pool.
- Snorkel on the coral reef.
- Go spelunking in a cave.
- Go fly fishing in a mountain stream.
- Enjoy the coolness of a forest.
- Go rafting through western canyons.
- Go mountain biking on a forest trail.
- Climb the rock wall.
- Hike a mountain trail.
- Relax in the wildflower garden.
- Fish in our country pond.
- Canoe through the swamp.
- Explore the desert.
- Stay at the campground (tent or trailer hook-ups), or in one of our log cabins scattered throughout the park.

Circle the correct answer.

1. The main idea of a travel brochure is to...
   a. entice people to visit.
   b. give you something fun to read.
   c. tell you how to plan your vacation.

2. To whom does this brochure appeal?
   a. people who love the city
   b. families who love outdoor adventure
   c. senior citizens seeking a relaxing vacation

3. List seven main attractions at the **Natural Wonders Park**.

   _____
   _____
   _____
   _____
   _____
   _____
   _____

Visit

Natural Wonders Park

for the
Perfect Vacation!

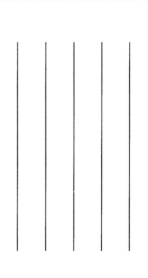

Name _____

 Name _____

From Oyster to Pearl

Many people admire the beauty of pearls, but do you know where they come from and how they are made? Most precious gems are dug up from the earth, but pearls are found inside the shells of oysters.

Oyster shells are lined with **nacre** (nā'kər), a special substance made by an organ called the **mantel**, which gives the shell its smooth, lustrous coating. Whenever a **foreign particle**, such as a grain of sand, piece of shell, or tiny parasite, enters the oyster's body, the mantel produces more nacre to cover the particle. More **layers** of nacre are built up around the particle until it is encased in its own shell. These shells can be pink, white, orange, gold, cream, or black.

If you were to cut a pearl in half, you would see layers almost like the rings of an onion. Each layer has **tiny crystals** of mineral substance. When light hits the surface it is split into rainbows of color which give pearls their **iridescence**. Pearls come in various **shapes**, but the most perfect and most valuable ones are round.

Pearls can be found in oysters in **natural** settings in the Persian Gulf and the South Pacific. Many oysters must be collected to find just a few pearls. Most pearls today are **cultured**. They are still grown inside oysters but in carefully controlled situations. Many young oysters are planted in oyster beds in shallow water. At the age of three they are brought to a **laboratory** where a tiny piece of nacre is inserted into each one. They are then replaced in protected beds where they are tended for **one to three years**. When the oysters are opened, a pearl is found in about one of every twenty shells. They are cleaned, washed, polished, and sent off to market.

Key words or phrases that help in understanding the main idea of this article appear in bold print. Write a paragraph that explains the main idea in your own words, using each key word or phrase.

_____

_____

_____

_____

_____

_____

_____

_____

_____

_____

Lost Colony

1. What is the main idea of this series of illustrations?
   a. Sir Walter Raleigh went to the New World in 1585.
   b. The settlement of Roanoke lasted for a short time before disappearing.
   c. The settlers of Roanoke made several trips back and forth from England.

2. What is the main idea of frames 1–4? _____

   _____

3. What is the main idea of frames 5–8? _____

   _____

4. What is the main idea of frames 9–12? _____

   _____

Try this: Write a conclusion to the Roanoke story by providing a solution to the settlers' disappearance.

Exploring the New World

The Norwegian Vikings were probably the first Europeans to explore the Americas. They were led by **Leif Ericson** in 1003, and explored Iceland, Greenland, and the northern coast of North America.

The next explorations of which we know didn't begin until the 1400s. In 1492, **Christopher Columbus** made his first famous voyage with the Niña, the Pinta, and the Santa Maria, sailing for Queen Isabella of Spain. He landed on an island off the coast of Florida, which he named San Salvador.

In 1497, **John Cabot** sailed from England to Newfoundland looking for a northern route to the Indies. He was followed by **Amerigo Vespucci** in 1507, who drew maps of the New World after sailing to the northern coast of South America and on to Hispaniola. The New World was named America after Amerigo Vespucci.

Ferdinand Magellan finally found a sailing route west to the Indies in 1519, by sailing around the southern tip of South America, across the Pacific Ocean, and on to the Spice Islands. After much difficulty, only one of his five ships finally returned to Spain.

Spaniard **Hernando Cortés** sailed to Mexico City in 1519, where he conquered the Aztecs and sent gold back to Spain. He was followed by other Spanish explorers also looking for riches. **Francisco Coronado** explored Texas in 1540, and discovered the Grand Canyon. In 1541, **Hernando de Soto** explored Florida, Alabama, Arkansas, and Mississippi. The members of his party were the first to see the Mississippi River.

Jacques Cartier was a Frenchman who explored the Atlantic coast and the St. Lawrence River in 1534. The land he claimed for France is now part of Canada.

Henry Hudson, an English navigator, explored New York Harbor for the Dutch in 1607–1610. He also sailed up the river now named after him, the Hudson.

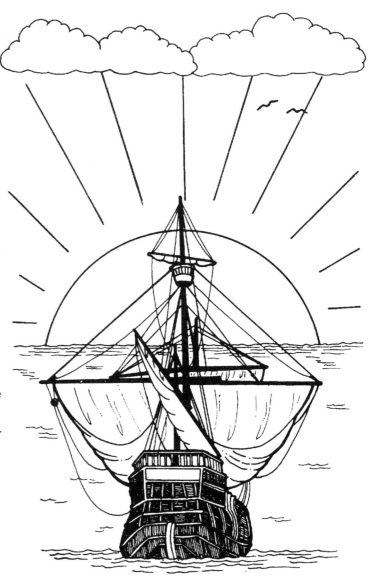

Exploring the New World (cont.)

The main idea of this exercise is to be able to transfer information you read onto maps and charts. Fill in the time line with the dates and names of each explorer listed in this article.

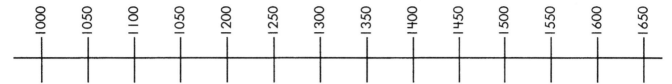

Complete the map by filling in each route with the correct explorer's name.

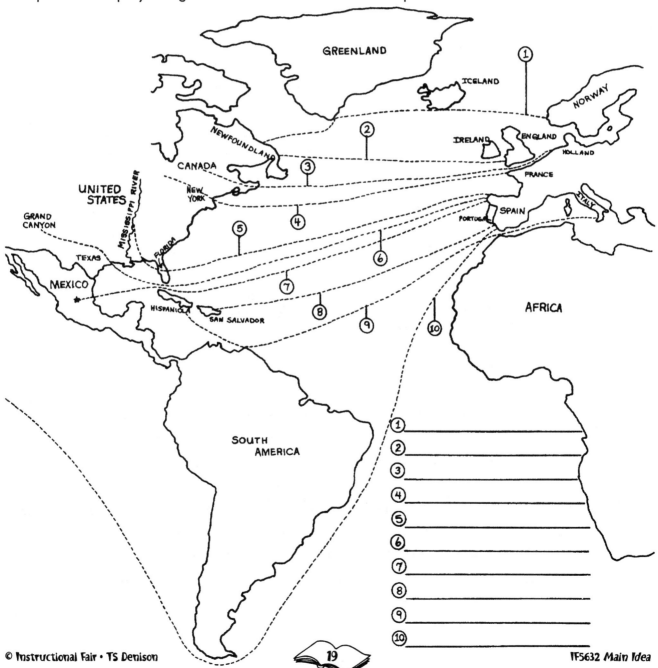

Will the Real Mark Twain Please Stand Up!

Have you ever heard of Samuel Clemens, Theodore Geisel, or Mary Ann Evans? Maybe you have heard of Mark Twain, Dr. Seuss, and George Eliot. These latter names are all the pen names (made-up names) that these famous people have used when authoring books.

Why would an author use a pen name? Sometimes it is done to protect privacy if the author is writing about something personal or controversial. Sometimes, if an author has written many books, he or she will use a different name to avoid flooding the market with many works under the same name. Some authors take pen names for other reasons as well.

Samuel Clemens spent much of his life on the Mississippi River. He even had a job piloting a boat on the river. Many of his books, including, *Huckleberry Finn, Tom Sawyer,* and *Life on the Mississippi,* take place on the river. When Samuel Clemens was a riverboat pilot, he learned to measure the depth of the river. A depth of two fathoms, or 12 feet (3.7 m), meant the river was naviga-

ble. This measurement was called "mark twain." Clemens felt it was the perfect name to use on his books.

Theodore Seuss Geisel wrote children's books full of silly names, invented words, and drawings of imaginary creatures. Maybe you have read *The Cat in the Hat* or *Green Eggs and Ham* or *Yertle the Turtle.* He used a pen name so that he could write books while being under contract for another job. His pen name helped him hide the fact that he was writing these books. In any case, Dr. Seuss is a very interesting name.

Mary Ann Evans lived in England in the 1800s and wrote most of her books about life in England. During this time, women were not accepted as professionals and writers. Mary Ann Evans chose the pen name George Eliot so that no one would discriminate against her.

George Sand, author of *A Grandmother's Tales*; George Orwell, author of *Animal Farm*; and Lewis Carroll, author of *Alice in Wonderland*, are all pen names. Can you find out their real names?

1. Write the main idea of this article in one sentence. _____

_____

2. What is the most likely reason Samuel Clemens changed his name? _____

_____

3. Why did Theodore Geisel use the name Dr. Seuss? _____

_____

4. Why did Mary Ann Evans use the name George Eliot when she wrote? _____

_____

5. If you were writing a book, what might you choose as your pen name? Why?

_____

_____

Mmmm, Mmmm Good!

1. According to the box, what is the main reason someone should buy this cereal?

    a. It is tasty and nutritious.

    b. You receive a free wildlife card.

    c. You can win a trip to Sea World.

2. What clues on the box help to tell you? _____

_____

_____

3. According to the cereal box, list three other reasons someone might buy this cereal.

_____

_____

_____

Paper Sculpture

Follow the instructions to build a paper cube which is similar in construction to the post and lintel style used by architects (two upright posts bridged by a horizontal beam).

1. Read all instructions before doing anything.
2. Cut out 12 paper strips that are 4" x 1" (approx. 10 cm x 2.5 cm).
3. Fold the strips in half lengthwise.

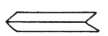

4. Glue or tape 4 strips together to form a square. Use just a small dab of glue or tape.

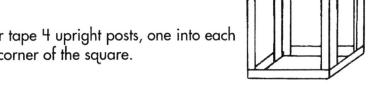

5. Glue or tape 4 upright posts, one into each inside corner of the square.

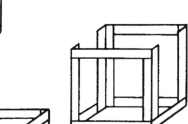

6. Glue or tape strips (lintels) across opposite sides, on top of the posts.

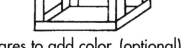

7. Glue or tape strips across the two remaining sides.

8. You may fill the openings with tissue paper squares to add color. (optional)

9. Combine your cube with those of other classmates, or make more of your own to build a tower or other structure.

10. Answer the following questions.
    If you follow steps 2–6, what will you end up with? _____
    What can be done with these shapes? _____
    What is the name of the building style on which this project is based? _____

    _____

11. What is the main idea of this reading selection? _____

    _____

12. Now start at step 2 and complete the project.

Name _____

A World of Color

I stand on the shore and gaze out over the ocean
at an endless sea of blue,
sometimes murky, sometimes clear, sparkling,
but always blue.
I plunge beneath the surface of blue,
my blinders are removed.
The blue has transformed into
myriad colors.
I wonder,
does a fish look at land and see only green?

Maybe people are the same.
I stand on my turf and look at my neighbor
and see only black or brown or yellow or red or white.
I wonder,
if I could dive beneath the surface
and walk around in his world,
what colors would be revealed?

Circle the letter of the BEST answer.

1. What do you think is the main reason the author wrote this poem?
   a. Colors are fascinating and revealing.
   b. One has to look beneath the surface to see what is really there.
   c. Underwater, everything is blue.

2. What two ideas is the author comparing?
   a. We see only the surface of the ocean until we dive under, and we see only the surface of a person until we take the time to get to know them.
   b. We see the ocean as a strange place, but fish think of it as their home.
   c. We are envious of our neighbor's land, and yet they are also envious of ours.

3. Think of an example from your life, a book, or a movie that shares the main idea of the poem. Write a paragraph about it.

_____

_____

_____

_____

_____

Name _____

Ancient Civilizations in the Americas

Three great ancient civilizations in the Americas were the Incan, the Aztec, and the Mayan. The Maya thrived between 1000 B.C. and 1542 A.D. and lived in the area we now know as Mexico's Yucatan Peninsula and Central America. The Incan empire was located along the west coast of South America in what are known today as Peru and Chile. Their empire lasted from about 1438 to about 1532 A.D. The Aztec lived during the 1400s in the area we know today as Mexico, with their capital city in the same place as modern-day Mexico City.

Agriculture was very important in these civilizations. The Aztec built chinampas, man-made island-gardens, in a lake which they accessed by canoe. The lake mud made great fertilizer. The Inca lived on mountain-sides. They terraced and used irrigation to grow crops. The Maya used a combination of these techniques, draining lowlands for soil, and utilizing highlands by terracing. The major crop for all three civilizations was maize (corn), which was ground into flour to make tortillas, tamales, and other foods.

These cultures worshipped many gods and goddesses. Quetzalcoatl was the Aztec god of nature. Chicomecoatl was the Aztec goddess of maize, and Huitzilopochtli was the war god of the Aztec. The Inca worshipped Inti, the sun. Chac was a Mayan god of rain. These ancients built elaborate temples for their gods. Some of them can still be seen today in the preserved ruins at Teotihaucan in Mexico City, Machu Picchu in Peru, and Tikal in Guatemala.

Both the Aztec and Inca conquered all the tribes around them, each culture incorporating all into their own mighty empire with a ruler over all. The Maya were different. There were many cities that shared the same culture and religion, but each city governed itself and had its own ruler.

The Maya left behind hieroglyphic writing that indicates they knew much about arithmetic and astronomy. They developed a very accurate calendar. The Inca are known for their fine stonework. They did not have any written language, but did use a quipu of knotted strings for counting. Although the Aztec are known for being fierce warriors, they left a huge sun stone which is actually a calendar.

What happened to these mighty empires? When the Spaniards came to the new world, they destroyed these cultures in their greediness for the gold of the new world. The Aztec believed Cortés was the god Quetzelcoatl, so they were easily conquered by him in 1519. In 1532, Pizarro overthrew the Inca. The Mayan empire lasted until 1542 when it, too, was conquered by the Spanish.

Name _____

Use with page 24.

Ancient Civilizations in the Americas (cont.)

One way to organize the main ideas from your reading is to construct an outline. Fill in the outline below with information from the article on the ancient civilizations in the Americas.

Title: _____

I. Maya
   A. Background Information
      1. date: _____
      2. location: _____
   B. Way of life
      1. Agriculture: _____
      2. Religion
         a. gods: _____

         _____

         b. temples: _____

         _____
      3. Government: _____
   C. Accomplishments
      1. _____
      2. _____
      3. _____
   D. End of Civilization
      1. conquered by:

         _____
      2. date: _____

II. Aztec
   A. Background Information
      1. date: _____
      2. location: _____
   B. Way of life
      1. Agriculture: _____
      2. Religion
         a. gods: _____

         _____

         b. temples: _____

         _____

3. Government: _____
C. Accomplishments
   1. _____
   2. _____
   3. _____
D. End of Civilization
   1. conquered by:

      _____
   2. date: _____

III. Inca
   A. Background Information
      1. date: _____
      2. location: _____
   B. Way of life
      1. Agriculture: _____
      2. Religion
         a. gods: _____

         _____

         b. temples: _____

         _____
      3. Government: _____
   C. Accomplishments
      1. _____
      2. _____
      3. _____
   D. End of Civilization
      1. conquered by:

         _____
      2. date: _____

Who's My Neighbor?

This is a logic puzzle. Logic puzzles help you develop thinking skills. Label each house with the correct person's name. Use the clues below to help you match each person with the correct house.

Use the grid to help you figure out this puzzle. Put an **X** in each box that could not possibly work and an **O** when you have a definite match. Once you record an **O**, place an **X** in all remaining boxes in that row and column. Clue #1 is done for you.

	1	2	3	4	5
Max				X	
Sam				X	
Kris				X	
Sue				X	
Cody	X	X	X	O	X

Clues

1. Cody lives in house #4.
2. Kris only has one neighbor.
3. Kris's neighbor is not Sam.
4. Sue's house is yellow.
5. Cody and Sam live next to Sue.
6. Max's house only has one window.
7. Max is Sam's neighbor.
8. Kris and Sue live two houses away from each other.
9. Sam's house is next to someone whose name starts with the same letter.

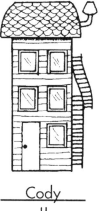

1   2   3   Cody 4   5

1. What was the main phrase to look for when organizing the houses?

_____

2. Give the number(s) of any clues that were not helpful. _____

Why were they not helpful? _____

_____

3. What is the main reason for doing this activity? _____

_____

Crazy Maze

A labyrinth is a maze of many confusing passageways. You may have played labyrinth games on the computer, but have you ever been inside a life-sized labyrinth and tried to find your way out?

In Greek mythology, there is a story about King Minos of Crete. He hired an inventor named Daedelus to build a large labyrinth where he imprisoned the Minotaur, a monster with the body of a man and the head of a bull. Each year, King Minos sacrificed seven young men and seven young maidens from Athens to the Minotaur by sending them into the labyrinth.

One year, the son of the king of Athens volunteered to go as a sacrifice. He was determined to kill the Minotaur and find his way out again so no more Athenians would have to be sacrificed. When he arrived on the island of Crete, King Minos' daughter, Ariadne fell in love with this man. She gave him a magic ball of string and told him to tie one end to the beginning of the maze so he could follow it back to find his way out. He did as she instructed and was able to find his way through the maze to the Minotaur, to kill him, and to rescue the thirteen others who had also been sacrificed that year.

Pick the correct word or phrase from the word boxes to fill in the blanks to tell the main idea of this story.

1. game
   maze
   computer
	2. Crete
	   Athens
	   Rome
		3. Minotaur
		   Ariadne
		   Daedelus

4. Daedelus
   Minos
   Ariadne
	5. daughter
	   Daedelus
	   Minotaur
		6. falling in love with Ariadne
		   following a string
		   remembering the way

Another word for a labyrinth is a (1) _____ . One of the most famous

labyrinths is found in (2) _____ . It was built by (3) _____

for King (4) _____ so he could keep the (5) _____ a

prisoner there. One young man found his way through the maze by (6) _____ .

See if you can find your way through this maze. If you go the correct way and pick up each letter you pass, you will find the name of the king's son from Athens. _____

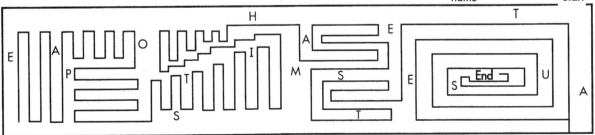

Name _____

A Brave Young Woman

(1) Imagine a 17-year-old girl going to her king and telling him she would like to lead his army to victory. Even more amazing, imagine the king agreeing with her. You may think this is a far-fetched story, but it really happened.

(2) The year was 1429. Joan of Arc was only 17 years old when she went to King Charles VII of France to tell him she had seen a vision and heard the voices of saints. God wanted her to free France from the English. She was to lead the French army in battle against the English at Orleans.

(3) The king wanted to test her to see if she really did possess extraordinary powers. He disguised himself and put one of his noble-men on the throne. Joan saw right through the disguise and went immediately to the real king with her request. He tested her again, and she was able to tell him what he prayed to God when he was alone. The king was convinced of her powers.

(4) Joan and her army went to Orleans in April of 1429, and defeated the English in only ten days. Charles had never been officially crowned king because the city of Reims, the coronation site for French kings, was in enemy territory. After the victory at Orleans, Joan escorted Charles to Reims, where he was crowned King on July 17, 1429.

(5) Joan wanted to free France completely from the English, so she went again into battle outside Paris. This time she was wound-ed and captured by the English. Rather than return her to the French in exchange for a ransom, as was the custom, the English kept her as a prisoner.

(6) Like the French, the English also believed Joan had supernatural powers. Where the French king thought they came from God, the English thought they were from the devil. Joan was charged with witchcraft by a French tribunal sympathetic to the English. She was found guilty and burned at the stake on May 30, 1431 in Rouen, France. Her ashes were thrown into the Seine River.

(7) Later, her family requested a new trial, and in 1456, she was found innocent. Although it was too late to save her life, she was declared a saint. Saint Joan of Arc is recognized on the date of her death, May 30.

Name _____

A Brave Young Woman (cont.)

Circle the answer that best tells the main idea of each numbered paragraph.

1. a. Something amazing might happen involving a 17-year-old girl and a king.
   b. This story is not possible; therefore, it is fiction.
   c. A story about a girl asking her king if she may lead his army is really true.

2. a. Joan of Arc led the French army in a battle at Orleans.
   b. Joan was 17 when she went to see the king.
   c. Joan heard voices telling her to lead the French in battle.

3. a. Joan was a good test-taker.
   b. The king tested Joan to see if what she claimed was true.
   c. She did not pass the first test, so she had to take another.

4. a. Joan was a military genius who defeated the English.
   b. The king was not officially crowned because the English held Reims.
   c. After defeating the English, Joan led the king to Reims to be officially crowned.

5. a. Joan liked wars, so she kept fighting until her capture by the English.
   b. In a battle near Paris, Joan was wounded, captured, and held prisoner by the English.
   c. The French army would not pay a ransom to the English to get Joan back.

6. a. Joan was tried for witchcraft and burned at the stake.
   b. There is a debate about whether Joan's power came from God or the devil.
   c. Joan's ashes were thrown into the Seine River.

7. a. Joan's family wanted to bring her back to life, so they requested a new trial.
   b. Joan was later found innocent and declared to be a saint.
   c. Joan is recognized on the date of her death.

Two Holidays

Each year, the citizens of the United States celebrate two holidays to remember service-men and -women who fought in wars to preserve citizens' freedom. On November 11, Veterans Day is celebrated, and on May 30, or the last Monday in May, Memorial Day.

November 11, 1918, was the day a treaty was signed between the Germans and the allied forces of the United States, France, Great Britain, Russia, and Italy, putting an end to World War I. This day was first called Armistice Day, but is now called Veterans Day. On that day, George Honey, an Australian journalist, asked the whole world to remain silent for two minutes as the treaty was signed. Even the radios were silent. The Great Silence is still observed in some Veterans Day celebrations.

Memorial Day began after the Civil War, when people began decorating the graves of soldiers who had died in the war. Although many claim to have started the tradition, Congress declared Waterloo, New York, the birthplace of Memorial Day when the whole community held a celebration on May 5, 1866. In 1868, the Grand Army of the Republic organized a ceremony at the National Cemetery in Arlington, Virginia. They called it Decoration Day because they decorated the graves of soldiers. The holiday stuck, but the name was changed to Memorial Day. On this day, many communities hold parades in remembrance of servicemen and -women who have given their lives for the freedom of the United States of America.

On the space in front of the following key words and phrases, write either **V** (Veterans Day) or **M** (Memorial Day) to show the correct holiday.

_____ May 30

_____ Great Silence

_____ George Honey

_____ Arlington Cemetery

_____ Decoration Day

_____ November 11

_____ decorated graves

_____ Civil War

_____ Armistice Day

_____ World War I

_____ Waterloo, NY

_____ Grand Army of the Republic

_____ parades

_____ signing of peace treaty

Saint Patrick

Read these three paragraphs about Saint Patrick's Day. Each one has a different purpose.

1. Today is a special day. Almost everyone is dressed in green. There are shamrocks everywhere. People are wearing buttons that say, "Kiss me, I'm Irish." Many of the big cities have parades. People are dancing to Irish music as they celebrate Saint Patrick's Day, March 17.

2. Even people who are not Irish love to celebrate Saint Patrick's Day, but many don't even know who Saint Patrick was. He was born and lived in England, which was then a part of the great Roman Empire, around 400 A.D. When Patrick was sixteen, pirates captured him and sold him as a slave in Ireland. After several years, he escaped and returned to England. He went to France and studied in a monastery. One night he had a dream telling him to return to Ireland. He returned as a bishop and built many churches, schools, and monasteries as he taught people about his faith. He also taught people to read and write. He was loved and respected by the Irish people and was made their patron saint. They celebrate his feast day on March 17.

3. On Saint Patrick's Day in the United States, people celebrate with parties and parades. In Ireland, however, it is a religious celebration. The people attend church and celebrate reverently. Patrick is credited with the conversion of the Irish to Christianity.

Write the number of the paragraph beside the sentence that tells the main idea of that paragraph.

_____ In Ireland, Saint Patrick's Day is a religious celebration and is observed differently than in the United States.

_____ Saint Patrick's Day is celebrated with many fun traditions such as wearing green clothing and shamrocks, participating in parades, and exhibiting Irish pride.

_____ Saint Patrick was a bishop who went to Ireland and built many churches. He was loved by the Irish people.

Write your own paragraph about Saint Patrick's Day, in which the main idea tells how you celebrate St. Patrick's Day at your home or school.

_____

_____

_____

_____

_____

Tape Recorders

Did you ever listen to a tape and wonder how music could be produced from that little cassette? Here is how it works:

Each cassette has a **supply reel** which contains a roll of **magnetic tape**. It also has a **take-up reel** to collect the tape after it runs through the recorder. A small motor turns a wheel called the **capstan**. A **pinch roller** pushes the magnetic tape against the capstan which pulls the tape past the **idler** (a wheel which helps control the speed and flow of the tape) and several heads to the take-up reel.

The heads are small electromagnets. The first head is the **erase head**. It produces a strong magnetic field to remove any previous recording. The second head is a **recording head**. A microphone converts sounds to electric currents. As the tape passes the head, which has a small gap, the magnetic field magnetizes iron oxide particles onto the tape in a pattern. The third head is a **playback head**. The magnetic patterns on the tape generate electric current which is picked up by an amplifier to strengthen the current and then sent on to the speaker to reproduce recorded sounds. The speed at which the tape passes the heads, inches per second, determines the quality of the tape. A faster speed produces a better quality tape.

The main idea of this article is to explain _____

_____ .

Label the diagram below with each part of the cassette tape as described in the article (supply reel, magnetic tape, take-up reel, capstan, pinch roller, idler, erase head, recording head, and playback head).

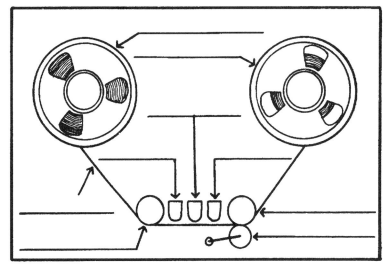

Legal and Binding Contract

When lawyers write legal contracts, they often use words that are not part of our everyday vocabulary. Read the contract to understand what is being offered to you and what your part of the bargain is. Each legal word in italics is followed by a more common word or phrase in parentheses.

It is hearby agreed that the *bearer* (owner) of this contract, who shall be named _____, hereafter named said student, shall be *entitled to* (given) privileges granted herein in accordance with the *contingencies* (rules) listed herein by _____ , hereafter named *grantor* (giver).

Contingencies:

- *Whereas* (if) said student completes all assignments *designated* (assigned) by grantor of this contract, and

- Whereas said student arrives in the classroom at the scheduled and appointed time, and

- Whereas said student *refrains* (keeps) from negative behavior in the classroom, including but not limited to, talking out of turn, *excessive* (over) use of pencil sharpening device, cruel behavior toward other classmates, in addition to any other behavior deemed unacceptable by grantor, then...

If it be *ascertained* (decided) by grantor that said student has successfully met contingencies above, grantor hereby commits to excusing student from one homework assignment without any *due consequences* (penalties).

Contract becomes *valid* (good) upon signatures of both said student and grantor.

Contract must be *redeemed* (traded in) within 30 days of date signed below or contract becomes *null and void* (no good).

Limitations (restrictions): Should said student *expressly* (purposefully) *violate contingencies* (break a rule) during that 30 day period, all *obligations* (promises) on the part of grantor shall *cease* and *terminate* (end).

_____	_____
Bearer signature	Date
_____	_____
Grantor signature	Date
_____	_____
Homework assignment excused	Date redeemed

1. What is the main purpose of the contract? _____
   _____

2. What do you have to do to redeem it? _____

3. What must your teacher do to make it valid? _____

4. When does it expire? _____

5. What are its limitations? _____
   _____

April Fools' Day

On the first of April we celebrate April Fools' Day. It's a fun day set aside to play jokes and make people laugh. How did it start? There are many theories.

(1)   There is a Roman myth from 2000 years ago about the goddess of grain and harvest. Ceres, and her daughter, Proserpina, were out picking flowers one spring day. The god of the dead, Pluto, saw Proserpina and thought her very beautiful. He kidnapped her to bring her to the land of the dead to be his queen. She did not want to go and cried out for help. Ceres heard her and began searching for her, but it was too late. Ceres could not enter the land of the dead. She had been fooled by Pluto. Some say this was the beginning of April fooling.

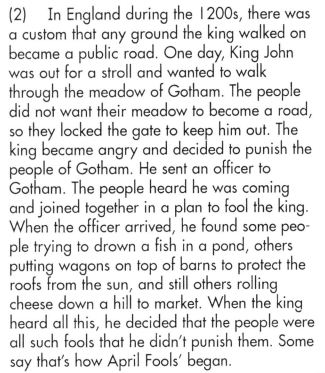

(2)   In England during the 1200s, there was a custom that any ground the king walked on became a public road. One day, King John was out for a stroll and wanted to walk through the meadow of Gotham. The people did not want their meadow to become a road, so they locked the gate to keep him out. The king became angry and decided to punish the people of Gotham. He sent an officer to Gotham. The people heard he was coming and joined together in a plan to fool the king. When the officer arrived, he found some people trying to drown a fish in a pond, others putting wagons on top of barns to protect the roofs from the sun, and still others rolling cheese down a hill to market. When the king heard all this, he decided that the people were all such fools that he didn't punish them. Some say that's how April Fools' began.

(3)   Until 1564, the New Year began on April 1. King Charles IX of France decided to switch to the Gregorian calendar, which began with January 1 as New Year's Day. Some people either didn't hear about the change or didn't like the change, and they continued to celebrate on April 1. Others began to play jokes on those who still celebrated on April 1. This fooling became a custom in France.

(4)   Some say there is a connection between April Fools' Day and catching fish. In the spring when all the young fish hatched, the streams were bursting with fish. These young fish were easily fooled by a hook and could be caught with little effort. French people who were easily fooled were called "poisson d'Avril," or April Fish. Even Napoleon Bonaparte was called "poisson d'Avril" for marrying his second wife on April 1.

(5)   In the 1700s, in Scotland, there was a tradition on April 1 called "hunting the gowk" (a cuckoo bird). Someone was chosen to deliver a message quite a distance away. Unbeknownst to the deliverer, the message read, "April 1, Hunt the gowk another mile." So when the message was read, the deliverer was sent on yet another errand. When he finally returned, having accomplished nothing, he'd find everyone laughing.

We don't know for sure exactly where or how April Fools' Day started, but it continues to be a fun day for pranksters in many countries around the world.

Name _____

Use with page 34.

April Fools' Day (cont.)

In each of the following, circle the letter of the sentence that best describes the main idea of each numbered paragraph. There are many statements that are true, but only one will answer the question asked.

What is the main idea of this reading?

a. The tradition of April Fools' Day was started in France.

b. There are several stories about how April Fools' Day started.

c. It is fun to play jokes on April Fools' Day.

1. a. Pluto may have played the first April Fools' Day trick by kidnapping Proserpina from Ceres.

   b. Ceres was the goddess of grain and harvest, and Pluto was the god of death.

   c. Proserpina was kidnapped and made queen of the land of the dead.

2. a. King John liked to walk and got angry when he couldn't walk where he wanted.

   b. The people of Gotham were very foolish, and so they were called the first April fools.

   c. April Fools' Day may have started when the people of Gotham fooled the king to avoid punishment.

3. a. The date of New Year's Day was changed from April 1 to January 1 in 1564.

   b. The king changed New Year's Day to January 1, and tricks were played on the people who still celebrated it on April 1.

   c. April Fools' Day used to be celebrated on January 1, instead of April 1.

4. a. There may be a connection between April fish and April Fools' Day, because the spring fish were easily fooled, as are people on April Fools' Day.

   b. In the spring, fish are easy to catch because there are so many of them.

   c. Napoleon Bonaparte was one of the first April fools because he got married on April 1.

5. a. The people in Scotland hunted a bird called a gowk, or cuckoo bird, for the first time each year on April 1.

   b. When someone read a message that said, "April 1, Hunt the gowk another mile," they made the person who delivered the note run.

   c. A traditional joke played on April Fools' Day in Scotland was to have someone run an errand called "hunting the gowk," in which the person is sent on errand after errand and never accomplishes anything.

Bill of Rights

When the founding fathers of the United States wrote the Constitution, they added ten amendments, called the Bill of Rights, to be sure certain rights would never be taken from the American people. Since that time, more amendments have been added. Here is the original Bill of Rights, as taken from the National Archives and Records Administration.

Amendment 1. Congress shall make no law respecting an establishment of religion, or prohibiting the free exercise thereof; or abridging the freedom of speech, or of the press; or the right of the people peaceably to assemble, and to petition the Government for a redress of grievances.

Amendment 2. A well regulated Militia, being necessary to the security of a free State, the right of the people to keep and bear Arms, shall not be infringed.

Amendment 3. No Soldier shall, in time of peace be quartered in any house, without the consent of the Owner, nor in time of war, but in a manner to be prescribed by law.

Amendment 4. The right of the people to be secure in their persons, houses, papers, and effects, against unreasonable searches and seizures, shall not be violated, and no Warrants shall issue, but upon probable cause, supported by Oath or affirmation, and particularly describing the place to be searched, and the persons or things to be seized.

Amendment 5. No person shall be held to answer for a capital, or otherwise infamous crime, unless on a presentment or indictment of a Grand Jury, except in cases arising in the land or naval forces, or in the Militia, when in actual service in time of War or public danger; nor shall any person be subject for the same offence to be twice put in jeopardy of life or limb; nor shall be compelled in any criminal case to be a witness against himself, nor be deprived of life, liberty, or property, without due process of law; nor shall private property be taken for public use, without just compensation.

Amendment 6. In all criminal prosecutions, the accused shall enjoy the right to a speedy and public trial, by an impartial jury of the State and district wherein the crime shall have been committed, which district shall have been previously ascertained by law, and to be informed of the nature and cause of the accusation; to be confronted with the witnesses against him; to have compulsory process for obtaining witnesses in his favor, and to have the Assistance of Counsel for his defence.

Amendment 7. In suits at common law, where the value in controversy shall exceed twenty dollars, the right of trial by jury shall be preserved, and no fact tried by a jury, shall be otherwise reexamined in any Court of the United States, than according to the rules of the common law.

Amendment 8. Excessive bail shall not be required, nor excessive fines imposed, nor cruel and unusual punishments inflicted.

Amendment 9. The enumeration in the Constitution, of certain rights, shall not be construed to deny or disparage others retained by the people.

Amendment 10. The powers not delegated to the United States by the Constitution, nor prohibited by it to the States, are reserved to the States respectively, or to the people.

Name _____

Use with page 36.

Bill of Rights (cont.)

Match each amendment in the Bill of Rights to the picture and caption that best tells the main idea of each by writing the number of the amendment on the line next to the caption.

Right to a fair trial _____

Freedom of religion, speech, press, peaceful assembly _____

Rights of the accused

_____

Conditions for quartering soldiers _____

Rules of construction of the constitution _____

Right to keep and bear arms _____

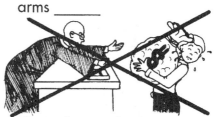

Protection against excessive bails, fines, and punishments _____

Powers delegated to the states _____

Right to a trial by jury _____

Regulations on search and seizure _____

Name _____

A Few of My Favorite Things

A survey was taken of a group of 200 fifth- and sixth- grade students, 100 girls and 100 boys. They were asked about their favorite things to see if there was a difference between the preferences of boys and girls. The graphs below show the results.

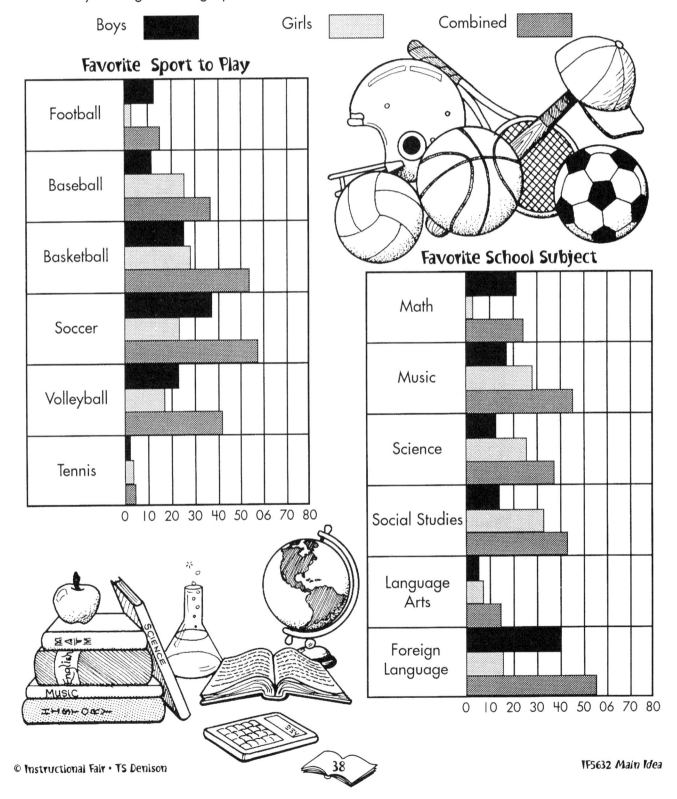

Boys ▮   Girls ▯   Combined ▨

Favorite Sport to Play

Football
Baseball
Basketball
Soccer
Volleyball
Tennis

0 10 20 30 40 50 06 70 80

Favorite School Subject

Math
Music
Science
Social Studies
Language Arts
Foreign Language

0 10 20 30 40 50 06 70 80

A Few of My Favorite Things (cont.)

1. What was the main reason for conducting this survey? _____

_____

2. What was the favorite in each category?

	boys	girls	combined
Sport	_____	_____	_____
Subject	_____	_____	_____

3. What was the least favorite in each category?

	boys	girls	combined
Sport	_____	_____	_____
Subject	_____	_____	_____

4. In which areas was there a significant difference between the boys' and the girls' favorite things? (significant means more than 2 or 3 out of 100)

_____

_____

5. Did the survey accomplish what it set out to do? _____

6. What are your favorites?

    Sport _____   Subject _____

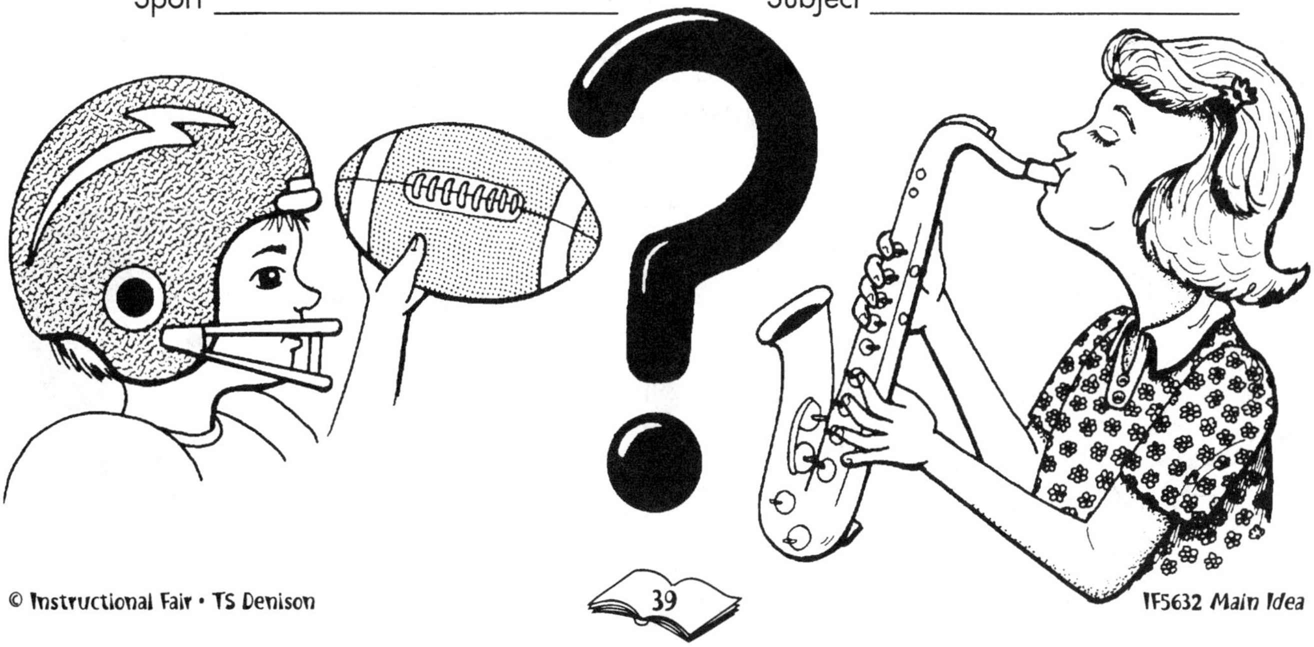

Use with page 41.

Let's Chat!

We live in a very mobile society, which means that friends and family are often moving away from each other. Fortunately, modern technology has made it easy to keep in touch. You no longer have to wait weeks for letters to travel back and forth, nor pay expensive phone bills. With Internet Relay Chat (IRC), you can communicate with people almost anywhere in the world for the cost of a local phone call to your Internet server. You can "chat" with each other by typing messages on your keyboard. Since typing takes a lot longer than talking, people who often use IRC have developed abbreviations which are commonly used and understood to help speed things up. Here are some of them:

BCNU—Be seeing you!	BTW—By the way
CUL8R—See you later	IMO—In my opinion
GMTA—Great minds think alike	J/K—Just kidding
LTNO—Long time no see	NP—No problem
ROTFL—Rolling on the floor laughing	THX—Thanks
RUOK—Are you OK?	TTFN—Ta-ta for now
WTG—Way to Go!	WYSIWYG—What you see is what you get!

Abbreviations are made up by shortening words like this: CN U RD THS (Can you read this)?

In a conversation, the tone of a person's voice or the expression on their face help you to better understand their meaning. On the Internet, you cannot see a face or hear a voice, but you can add emotional expression to your messages by using "emoticons" (emotional icons). These are made by combining various symbols such as a colon, hyphen, and parenthesis to make a smiley face :-) . You may have to turn it sideways to recognize it. Here are some others:

:-))	very happy	I-O	yawn
:-* or **	kiss	:-@	screaming
:'-(	crying	:-D	laughing out loud
%-)	confused	:-((	very sad
;-)	winking	:-||	angry
:-(	sad	:-/	undecided

Name _____

Use with page 40.

Let's Chat! (cont.)

Circle the letter of the best answer.

1. The main idea of this article is to...
   a. tell you how to use the Internet.
   b. introduce Internet Relay Chat.
   c. teach you a new language.

2. Users of IRC use abbreviations...
   a. to have their own private language that no one else can understand.
   b. to be able to communciate faster while typing.
   c. because they don't know how to spell words correctly.

3. Emotions on IRC ...
   a. are impossible to show because it's all typed words.
   b. are not necessary, since you can type words to mean exactly what you want to say.
   c. can be shown using emoticons such as the smiley face.

Here is a chat message to you. Can you read it?

IMO it's TM 4 U 2 HV SM FN with IRC.
SND a message 2 a FRND & HV HM RSPND. TTFN.   :-))

Send your message here.

To: _____
From: _____
_____
_____
_____
_____
_____
_____
_____
_____
_____

Answer Key

Main Idea—Grades 5–6

The Enormous, Endangered Grizzly Bear

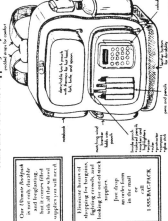

[1] Grizzly bears stand up to three and a half feet (1.0675 m) tall at the shoulders and are from six to seven feet (1.83 to 2.135 m) long. They weigh between 325 and 850 pounds (148 and 386 kg). Their name comes from their frost-tipped dorsal hairs, and their color can vary from dark brown to nearly black to pale yellow.

[2] A grizzly bear's habitat must include plenty of space; they range up to 150 square miles (390 sq km). They prefer a subalpine climate near a body of water where they can find potential den sites. This habitat must also provide diverse and abundant food. Grizzly bears eat berries, pine nuts, grasses, herbs, and sedges, but over half their diet is meat. This comes from carrion, small rodents, and malnourished game, which is easy to hunt. They also like to raid garbage dumps. Grizzlies must eat enough to store up fat during hibernation.

[3] The breeding season for grizzly bears is from mid-May to mid-July. A female grizzly reaches sexual maturity at about four and a half years, and a male at three and a half years, while males may mate several times during one season. Grizzlies have a six month gestation period. Once a female becomes pregnant, she begins to eat more to store up fat for herself and her cubs. She will gain up to 400 pounds (182 kg). She begins to prepare her den between October and November.

[4] Grizzly cubs are born between January and March. They will emerge from their den with their mother anywhere from late March to early May. Cubs begin to eat solid food at six

months of age when their mothers teach them to hunt and forage. Fifty percent of grizzly cubs die during their first year due to malnutrition and attack by other animals. If they survive, they will den with their mothers for two winters. Grizzly bears live about 15 years, although some have been known to live for 30.

[5] The grizzly bear population is endangered. They like the same fertile areas that farmers and ranchers like. Ranchers see them as a threat to their livestock and will often shoot them. The grizzly bear habitat is shrinking because of the expansion of residential and recreational areas. Only one percent of their original historic range exists today in the lower 48 states. Because their habitat is shrinking, their populations have become isolated and their gene pool limited.

[6] Conservationists are working to improve the situation for grizzly bears. They are trying to claim back land for habitat. They tag the bears so they can follow their movements and learn more about what they need to survive. Conservationists are trying to reintroduce grizzlies into the Northern Rockies. This will increase the gene flow with the Yellowstone bears. These activists need support from concerned citizens who care about the survival of the great grizzly bear.

Page 4

The Enormous, Endangered Grizzly Bear (cont.)

Circle the answer that best tells the main idea of each numbered paragraph. Be sure to read all answers carefully before choosing one. There may be several true answers, but only one tells the main idea.

1. The main idea is ...
   a. to give a description of the grizzly bear. *(circled)*
   b. to give heights of grizzly bears
   c. to explain the name origin of the grizzly bear

2. a. A grizzly bear's habitat must have nuts, berries, and plenty of meat
   b. A grizzly bear's habitat must be 150 square miles (390 sq km)
   c. A grizzly bear's habitat must have plenty of space, the right kind of food, and potential den sites. *(circled)*

3. a. Several grizzly males can mate with a single female
   b. Grizzly females gain weight and find a den to prepare for childbirth. *(circled)*
   c. Grizzly bears follow specific breeding patterns.

4. a. Grizzly bears can live to be 30 years old
   b. A grizzly bear's survival can be uncertain, but they are capable of having a long life. *(circled)*
   c. Fifty percent of cubs die during their first year

5. a. Grizzly bears are endangered because of various threats to their survival *(circled)*
   b. Grizzly bears are endangered by ranchers
   c. Grizzly bear habitats are shrinking because of increased recreation and residential areas

6. a. Various efforts are being made to recover the grizzly bear population *(circled)*
   b. Grizzly bear populations should be reintroduced to their old habitat areas.
   c. Conservationists tag grizzly bears to study them.

7. The main idea of the whole article is ...
   a. about grizzly bear habitats.
   b. about grizzly bear predators.
   c. about grizzly bears and what is happening to them. *(circled)*

Page 5

The Ultimate Backpack

Read the magazine advertisement. Then, answer the questions below.

Make back-to-school shopping easy!

Our *Ultimate Backpack* is not only durable and longlasting, but it comes filled with all the school supplies you will need.

Eliminate hours of shopping for bargains, fighting crowds, and looking for out-of-stock supplies.

Just drop an order form in the mail or call 1-555-BAC-PACK.

1. What is the main selling point of this backpack?
   It eliminates hours spent shopping.

2. What are two reasons the advertisement gives to support this idea?
   all the school supplies you will need.
   order by mail or call.

3. To whom would this advertisement appeal?
   people who are busy or who don't like to shop

4. How can you receive this product?
   drop an order form in the mail
   or call 1-555-BAC-PACK

Page 6

Pen Pals

Dear Jessica,

Hi, how are you? I haven't seen you for such a long time. I probably wouldn't recognize you. Did you say you got your hair cut short? Mine is still long, but it's permed now.

Guess what! The real reason I'm writing this letter is to tell you that I'm coming back to visit on the third weekend of March. My Dad has a business trip planned only with you instead of at the hotel with okay with your family? I can stay with you on Friday and leave Sunday. That way I can go to school with you on him. Please write back and let me know if that's okay. We'll come in on Thursday to see everyone. Did anybody else move away? Is Clint still in your class? Does he have another girlfriend, or do you think he still likes me? I'm so excited, I can't wait to see you. Write back soon!

Your best friend for always,

Heather

Write a letter back to Heather, responding to the main point of her letter.

Answers will vary, but must repond to the trip Heather will be taking.

Page 7

IF5632 Main Idea

Wetlands

Wetlands are low areas that are soaked with water. They can consist of freshwater or saltwater. They can be found on the coast or inland. Wetlands include marshes, swamps, lagoons, bogs, and prairie potholes.

Wetlands are often thought of as soggy pieces of ground that are good for nothing except mosquito breeding. About a half-million acres per year are destroyed for agricultural use, malls, or housing developments. Since scientists have discovered that wetlands are a very valuable resource, many people today are trying to protect them from further destruction.

Wetlands provide shelter for many different animals including fish, birds, and mammals. Many of these animals could be left homeless and could face extinction without wetlands. Because the plants provide good cover, wetlands are a great breeding and nesting ground for the animals.

Migratory birds use the wetlands for a resting place as they travel back and forth between summer and winter habitats. As these birds follow the same route year after year, they depend on the wetlands that they once have used for centuries. Can you imagine what would happen if they were ready to stop and rest for the night and found a mall instead of their wetlands?

The plants that grow in a wetland area are an important part of the food web. They provide nutrient rich food for all the herbivores and omnivores that live there. They, in turn, provide food for the carnivores.

Wetlands also help to prevent flooding. They provide a place for the excess water to spill out and be soaked up like a sponge. In times of heavy rains, there is a place for the excess water to sit until it can flow out into streams.

The natural sponges also act as strainers to sift mud and allow silt to settle. They trap sewage waste and allow silt to settle. The streams that flow out of wetlands are cleaner than when the water first arrives into them.

Wetlands also act as a filter to clean toxins from the water. They help in the decomposition of harmful substances. The plants in the wetlands help keep nutrient concentrations from reaching toxic levels. In some areas where wetlands have been filled, too many nitrates are entering the water, making it unsafe to drink. Because plants produce oxygen in the process of photosynthesis, plants in the wetlands also mix oxygen into the water. Wetlands are a very valuable resource. Let's do all we can to preserve them.

Page 10

Editorials

An editorial page in a newspaper gives people an opportunity to express their opinion on an issue in a public forum. Here are two editorials, each expressing a different opinion of professional basketball players.

Dear Editor,
I think that many people in our country give too much glory to basketball players. They make millions of bucks for playing a basketball game. They get to wear expensive name-brand shoes and clothing which they don't even have to buy, and they are the ones who can afford them. They only work part of the year, and then they go on strike demanding more money. They are greedy and selfish. Sure, some of the athletes donate money to charity, but what they give is only a small fraction of what they keep for themselves. Tickets are so expensive, most kids can't afford to go to a game. Why should we continue to pay them to have fun? Basketball is just a game. Instead of worshiping someone else for playing basketball, we should be out playing ourselves.
Fed-up in Fennville

Dear Editor,
Let's hear it for the professional B'ball players! American kids need something good to believe in. Many athletes weren't always rich. Many of them worked very hard to get where they are today. They give all kids hope that maybe someday we could be there too. The athletes inspire us to try harder and to be the best we can, just as they are. They inspire us to get off the couch, and to play ball, have fun, and exercise. They are heroes and positive role models. We, in America, are lucky to have these athletes to look up to.
Pleased in Petoskey

Circle the correct answer.
1. Fed up in Fennville thinks professional basketball players are...
   (a) greedy and selfish.   b. giving kids hope.   c. inspiring youngsters.
2. Pleased in Petoskey thinks professional basketball players...
   a. are paid too much.
   b. donate money to charity.
   (c) inspire kids and give them hope.
3. Write F (fed up in Fennville) or P (Pleased in Petoskey) to identify the source of each detail.
   F wear expensive clothing   P give hope
   P exercise   F greedy and selfish
   F get too much glory   P make millions
   F basketball is just a game   P work hard

(Try this: Write your own editorial expressing your opinion of professional athletes.)
Page 9

Message

You have just arrived at the home of some friends and found this note on the door with your name on it. Decode the rebus to discover the message. Then answer the question.

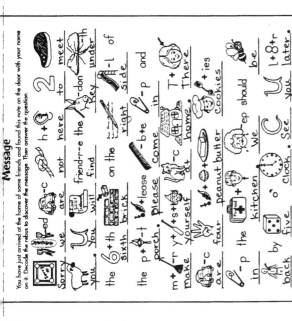

Sorry we are not here to meet you. You will find friend-re the key under the 6th brick on the right side of the p+d-t porch. Please come in and make yourself at home. -c-p the four peanut butter cookies in the kitchen. We -ep should be back by five o'clock. See you later.

What is the main idea of your friends' message? We should let ourselves in with the key and enjoy some cookies. They will be home at 5:00.

Page 8

Wetlands (cont.)

Each picture in the web below represents one of the attributes of the wetlands. On or next to each picture, write a phrase describing the main reason that picture represents a wetland.

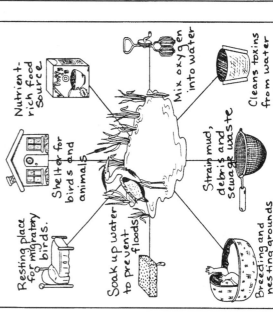

Resting place for migratory birds.
Nutrient-rich food source
Shelter for birds and animals
Mix oxygen into water
Soak up water to prevent floods
Strain mud, debris and sewage waste
Cleans toxins from water
Breeding and nesting grounds

Page 11

Today's News

Hurricane Hits Hard

Hurricane Harold hit Honolulu, Hawaii, yesterday at 5:30 A.M. Tourists and residents had to evacuate hotels and homes as water levels rose to dangerous heights. Hotel Hono was hit the hardest. Windows in the lobby were broken as water gushed in, washing away chairs, tables, and hotel records. Only one of the stately palms of the entrance still stands. Fortunately, everyone was evacuated in time. There were no fatalities. Only minor injuries were reported.

Pet Problems

The town council of Pleasantville met yesterday to discuss the problems caused by pets in the city parks.

"People need to take responsibility for their pets," claimed one citizen. "The pets are running wild and producing piles of poo in the park."

"These animals present a danger to children who want to pet them. Please do something," pleaded another.

"Our animals are cooped up all day and need a place to run. The park is the only safe space," protested a pet owner.

After listening to all arguments, the mayor proposed a solution. "Anyone bringing a pet to the park must use a leash to keep it restrained. They must also carry a bag and travel to dispose of any waste left by the pet. A one-fourth acre area of the park will be fenced off so owners can release their pets to run there without endangering the children who are playing in the park."

The proposal was unanimously approved by all those present and will go into effect next week.

Falcons Flog Pirates

The Fairview Falcons are having a fabulous football season. On Saturday, they defeated their opponents, the Pleasantville Pirates, 52-19. The Falcons' four touchdowns were scored by the flying running back Frank Fernhide. The other three were scored on fantastic passes from quarterback Fred Foldsover. All extra points and the final field goal were converted from the foot of Farley Fitzgerald. After the victory, the fans cheered, running onto the field.

Town Pride

The Eco Club of Redville will be sponsoring a "Be Proud of Your town" clean-up day this Saturday from 8:00-4:00. They will pick up any recyclable waste left at the curb. Please have waste separated into boxes for paper, metal, glass, and plastic. There are volunteers to help senior citizens. If you would like Angie at 555-5555 before Friday afternoon. Let's all work together to make our town "The Best Around."

Page 12

Today's News (cont.)

Circle the correct answer concerning these news articles.

Hurricane Hits Hard
What is the main message of this article?
   a. A hurricane hit Honolulu.
   (b) Hotel Hono was ruined by a hurricane.
   c. Tourists and residents were evacuated.
   d. No fatalities occurred.

Pet Problems
The conflict is between...
   a. dogs and kids.
   (b) the mayor and the citizens.
   c. dog owners and other citizens.
   d. pets and city parks.

Complete the following.
Falcons Flog Pirates
Who won the game? the Fairview Falcons
Who scored the most touchdowns? Frank Fernhide
Town Pride
On what day and at what time is the clean up being held? Saturday - 8am-4pm
Where should waste be left? at the curb
Whom should you call for assistance? Angie-555-5555

Extra, Extra!
Find an article in your local newspaper. Write the main idea of the article in one or two sentences, including the who, what, when, where, and why. Give a news report to your class.
Answers will vary.

Page 13

From Oyster to Pearl

Many people admire the beauty of pearls, but do you know where they come from and how they are made? Most precious gems are dug up from the earth, but pearls are found inside the shells of oysters.

Oyster shells are lined with **nacre** (nā'kər), a special substance made by an organ called the mantle, which gives the shell its smooth, lustrous coating. Whenever an oyster's shell is split in half, piece of shell, or tiny parasite, enters the oyster's body, the mantle produces more nacre to cover the particle. More layers of nacre are built up around the particle until it is encased in its own shell. These shells can be pink, white, orange, gold, cream, or black.

If you were to cut a pearl in half, you would see layers almost like the rings of an onion. Each layer has tiny crystals of mineral substance. When light hits the surface it is split into rainbows of color which give pearls their **iridescence**. Pearls come in various shapes, but the most perfect and most valuable ones are round.

Pearls can be found in oysters in natural settings in the Persian Gulf and the South Pacific. Many oysters must be collected to find just a few pearls. Most pearls today are **cultured**. They are still grown inside oysters but in carefully controlled situations. Many young oysters are planted in oyster beds in shallow water. At the age of three they are brought to a laboratory where a tiny piece of nacre is inserted into each one. They are then replaced in protected beds where they are tended for one to three years. When the oysters are opened, a pearl is found in about one of every twenty shells. They are cleaned, washed, polished, and sent off to market.

Key words or phrases that help in understanding the main idea of this article appear in bold print. Write a paragraph that explains the main idea in your own words, using each key word or phrase.

Answers will vary, but must include all terms above in bold print.

Page 16

Exploring the New World (cont.)

The main idea of this exercise is to be able to transfer information you read onto maps and charts. Fill in the time line with the dates and names of each explorer listed in this article.

Complete the map by filling in each route with the correct explorer's name.

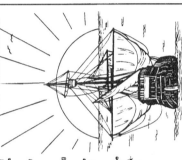

① Leif Ericson
② John Cabot
③ Jacques Cartier
④ Henry Hudson
⑤ Hernando de Soto
⑥ Francisco Coronado
⑦ Hernando Cortés
⑧ Christopher Columbus
⑨ Amerigo Vespucci
⑩ Ferdinand Magellan

Page 19

Visit Natural Wonders Park
for the Perfect Vacation!

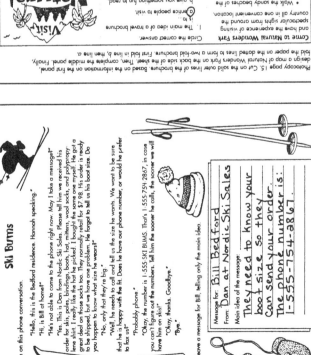

Photocopy page 15. Cut on the solid outer lines of the brochure. Based on the information on the first panel, design a map of Natural Wonders Park on the back side of the sheet. Then, complete the middle panel. Finally, fold the paper on the dotted lines to form a two-fold brochure. First fold in line b, then line a.

Come to Natural Wonders Park...

1. The main idea of this brochure is to:
   a. give you how to plan your vacation.
   b. give you something fun to read.
   (c.) entice people to visit. ✓

2. To whom does this brochure appeal?
   a. people who love the city
   (b.) families who love outdoor adventure ✓
   c. senior citizens seeking a relaxing vacation.

3. List seven main attractions of the Natural Wonders Park.
   • Explore a hide pool.
   • Snorkel on the coral reef.
   • Go spelunking in a cave.
   • Go fishing in a mountain stream.
   • Enjoy the coolness of a forest.
   • Go rafting through western canyons.
   • Go mountain biking on a forest trail.
   • Climb the rock wall.
   • Hike a mountain trail.
   • Relax in the wildflower garden.
   • Fish in our country pond.
   • Canoe through the swamp.
   • Explore the desert.
   • Stay at the campground (tent or trailer hook-ups), or in one of our log cabins scattered throughout the park.

Answers may vary, but should come from list at left.

Page 15

Exploring the New World

The Norwegian Vikings were probably the first Europeans to explore the Americas. They were led by Leif Ericson in 1003, and explored Iceland, Greenland, and the northern coast of North America.

The next explorations of which we know didn't begin until the 1400s. In 1492, Christopher Columbus made his first famous voyage with the Niña, the Pinta, and the Santa Maria, sailing for Queen Isabella of Spain. He landed on an island off the coast of Florida, which he named San Salvador.

In 1497, John Cabot sailed from England to Newfoundland looking for a northern route to the Indies. He was followed by Amerigo Vespucci in 1507, who drew maps of the New World after sailing to the northern coast of South America and on to Hispaniola. The New World was named America after Amerigo Vespucci.

Ferdinand Magellan finally found a sailing route west to the Indies in 1519, by sailing around the southern tip of South America, across the Pacific Ocean, and on to the Spice Islands. After much difficulty, only one of his five ships finally returned to Spain.

Spaniard Hernando Cortés sailed to Mexico City in 1519, where he conquered the Aztecs and sent gold back to Spain. He was followed by other Spanish explorers also looking for riches. Francisco Coronado explored Texas in 1540, and discovered the Grand Canyon in 1541. Hernando de Soto explored Florida, Alabama, Arkansas, and Mississippi. The members of his party were the first to see the Mississippi River.

Jacques Cartier was a Frenchman who explored the Atlantic coast and the St. Lawrence River in 1534. The land he claimed for France is now a part of Canada.

Henry Hudson, an English navigator, explored New York Harbor for the Dutch in 1607-1610. He also sailed up the river now named after him, the Hudson.

Page 18

Ski Bums

Listen in on this phone conversation.

"Hello, this is the Bedford residence. Hannah speaking."

"Hi, is Bill at home?"

"He's not able to come to the phone right now. May I take a message?"

"Yes. This is Dan from Nordic Ski Sales. Please tell him we received his order for skis, poles, bindings, boots, hat, mittens, wool socks, and polypropylene shirt. I really like the hat he picked. I bought the same one myself. He got a great deal on those socks too. They normally retail for $7.98. His order is ready to be shipped, but we have one more problem. He forgot to tell us his boot size. Do you happen to know what size he wears?"

"No, only that they're big."

"Well, he needs to call and tell us the size he wants. We want to be sure that he is happy with the fit. Does he have our phone number, or would he prefer to fax us?"

"Probably phone."

"Okay, the number is 1-555-SKI BUMS. That's 1-555-754-2867, in case you can't figure out the numbers. Tell him the sooner he calls, the sooner we will have him on skis!"

"Okay, thanks. Goodbye."

"Bye."

Please leave a message for Bill, telling only the main idea.

Message for: Bill Bedford
From: Dan at Nordic Ski Sales
Main idea of the message:
They need to know your boot size so they can send your order. The phone number is: 1-555-754-2867.

Page 14

Lost Colony

1. What is the main idea of this series of illustrations?
   a. Sir Walter Raleigh went to the New World in 1585.
   (b) The settlement of Roanoke lasted for a short time before disappearing. ✓
   c. The settlers of Roanoke made several trips back and forth from England.

2. What is the main idea of frames 1-4? The ship finds land and returns again after getting supplies.

3. What is the main idea of frames 5-8? A settlement is established but John White returns for supplies.

4. What is the main idea of frames 9-12? Delayed by a war, John White returns to find no trace of the Roanoke settlement.

(Try this: Write a conclusion to the Roanoke story by providing a solution to the settlers' disappearance.)

Page 17

Will the Real Mark Twain Please Stand Up!

Have you ever heard of Samuel Clemens, Theodore Geisel, or Mary Ann Evans? Maybe you have heard of Mark Twain, Dr. Seuss, and George Eliot. These latter names are all the pen names (made-up names) that these famous people have used when authoring books.

Why would an author use a pen name? Sometimes it is done to protect privacy if the author is writing about something personal or controversial. Sometimes, if an author has written many books, he or she will use a different name to avoid flooding the market with many works under the same name. Some authors take pen names for other reasons as well.

Samuel Clemens spent much of his life on the Mississippi River. He even had a job piloting a boat on the river. Many of his books, including, Huckleberry Finn, Tom Sawyer, and Life on the Mississippi, take place on the river. When Samuel Clemens was a riverboat pilot, he learned to measure the depth of the river. A depth of two fathoms, or 12 feet (3.7 m), meant the river was navigat-

ble. This measurement was called "mark twain." Clemens felt it was the perfect name to use on his books.

Theodore Seuss Geisel wrote children's books full of silly names, invented words, and drawings of imaginary creatures. Maybe you have read The Cat in the Hat or Green Eggs and Ham or Yertle the Turtle. He used a pen name so that he could write books while being under contract for another job. His pen name helped him hide the fact that he was writing these books. In any case, Dr. Seuss is a very interesting name.

Mary Ann Evans lived in England in the 1800s and wrote most of her books about life in England. During this time, women were not accepted as professionals and writers. Mary Ann Evans chose the pen name George Eliot so that no one would discriminate against her.

George Sand, author of A Grandmother's Tales, George Orwell, author of Animal Farm, and Lewis Carroll, author of Alice in Wonderland, are all pen names. Can you find out their real names?

1. Write the main idea of this article in one sentence. Some authors use pen names when they write for various reasons.
2. What is the most likely reason Samuel Clemens changed his name? He loved the river and decided to use a riverboat term.
3. Why did Theodore Geisel use the name Dr. Seuss? He was still under contract with another publisher.
4. Why did Mary Ann Evans use the name George Eliot when she wrote? She did not want to be discriminated against.
5. If you were writing a book, what might you choose as your pen name? Why? Answers will vary.

Page 20

Mmmm, Mmmm Good!

[cereal box illustration "Under the Sea — The tastiest, most nutritious cereal you'll ever eat."]

1. According to the box, what is the main reason someone should buy this cereal?
   a. It is tasty and nutritious.
   b. You receive a free wildlife card.
   c. You can win a trip to Sea World.

2. What clues on the box help to tell you? 8essential vitamins, calcium, natural sweeteners, mother approved, real fruit flavors

3. According to the cereal box, list three other reasons someone might buy this cereal? milk turns blue, can win wildlife cards, can give to "Save the whales", win a trip to Sea World.

Page 21

Paper Sculpture

Follow the instructions to build a paper cube which is similar in construction to the post and lintel style used by architects (two upright posts bridged by a horizontal beam).

1. Read all instructions before doing anything.
2. Cut out 12 paper strips that are 4" x 1" (approx. 10 cm x 2.5 cm).
3. Fold the strips in half lengthwise.
4. Glue or tape 4 strips together to form a square.
5. Glue or tape 4 upright posts, one into each inside corner of the square.
6. Glue or tape strips (lintels) across opposite sides, on top of the posts.
7. Glue or tape strips across the two remaining sides.
8. You may fill the openings with tissue paper squares to add color (optional).
9. Combine your cube with those of other classmates, or make more of your own to build a tower or other structure.
10. Answer the following questions.
   If you follow steps 2–6, what will you end up with? a cube
   What can be done with these shapes? build towers and structures
   What is the name of the building style on which this project is based? post and lintel
11. What is the main idea of this reading selection? to give directions on how to build a cube.
12. Now start at step 2 and complete the project.

Page 22

A World of Color

I stand on the shore and gaze out over the ocean
an endless sea of blue,
sometimes murky, sometimes clear, sparkling,
but always blue.
I plunge beneath the surface of blue,
my blinders are removed,
the blue has transformed into
myriad colors.
I wonder,
does a fish look at land and see only green?
Maybe people see the same.
I stand on my turf and look at my neighbor
and see only black or brown or yellow or red or white.
I wonder,
if I could dive beneath the surface
and walk around in his world,
what colors would be revealed?

Circle the letter of the BEST answer.

1. What do you think is the main reason the author wrote this poem?
   a. Colors are fascinating and revealing.
   b. One has to look beneath the surface to see who is really there.
   c. Underwater, everything is blue.

2. What is the author comparing?
   a. We see only the surface of the ocean until we dive under, and we see only the surface of a person until we take the time to get to know them.
   b. Colors under the sea are a strange place, but fish think of it as their home.
   c. We are envious of our neighbor's land, and yet they are also envious of ours.

3. Think of an example from your life, a book, or a movie that shares the main idea of the poem. Write a paragraph about it. Answers will vary.

Page 23

Ancient Civilizations in the Americas

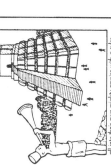

Three great ancient civilizations in the Americas were the Incan, the Aztec, and the Mayan. The Maya thrived between 1000 B.C. and 1542 A.D. and lived in the area we now know as Mexico's Yucatan Peninsula and Central America. The Incan empire was located along the west coast of South America in what are known today as Peru and Chile. Their empire lasted from about 1438 to about 1532 A.D. The Aztec lived during the 1400s in the area we know today as Mexico, with their capital city in the same place as modern-day Mexico City.

Agriculture was very important in these civilizations. The Aztec built chinampas, man-made island gardens, in a lake which they accessed by canoe. The lake mud made great fertilizer. The Inca lived on mountainsides. They terraced and used irrigation to grow crops. The Maya used a combination of these techniques, draining lowlands for soil, and utilizing highlands by terracing. The major crop for all three civilizations was maize (corn), which was ground into flour to make tortillas, tamales, and other foods.

These cultures worshipped many gods and goddesses. Quetzalcoatl was the Aztec god of nature. Chicomecoatl was the Aztec goddess of maize, and Huitzilopochtli was the war god of the Aztec. The Inca worshipped Inti, the sun. Chac was a Mayan god of rain. These ancients built elaborate temples for their gods. Some of them can still be seen today in the preserved ruins at Teotihuacan in Mexico City, Machu Picchu in Peru, and Tikal in Guatemola.

Both the Aztec and Inca conquered all the tribes around them, each culture incorporating

all into their own mighty empire with a ruler over all. The Maya were different. There were many cities that shared the same culture and religion, but each city governed itself and had its own ruler.

The Maya left behind hieroglyphic writing that indicates they knew much about arithmetic and astronomy. They developed a very accurate calendar. The Inca are known for their fine stonework. They did not have any written language, but did use a quipu of knotted strings for counting. Although the Aztec are known for being fierce warriors, they left a huge sun stone which is actually a calendar.

What happened to these mighty empires? When the Spaniards came to the new world, they destroyed these cultures in their greediness for the gold of the new world. The Aztec believed Cortés would be the god Quetzalcoatl, so they were easily conquered by him in 1519. In 1532, Pizarro conquered the Inca. The Mayan empire lasted until 1542 when it, too, was conquered by the Spanish.

Page 24

Ancient Civilizations in the Americas (cont.)

One way to organize the main ideas from your reading is to construct an outline. Fill in the outline below with information from the article on the ancient civilizations in the Americas.

Title: Ancient Civilizations in the Americas

I. Maya
   A. Background Information
      1. date: 1000 B.C. – 1542 A.D.
      2. location: Yucatan and C. America
   B. Way of life
      1. Agriculture: Combination of techniques
      2. Religion
         a. gods: Chac – god of rain
         b. temples: Tikal in Guatemala
   C. Accomplishments
      1. hieroglyphics
      2. arithmetic/astronomy
      3. accurate calendar
   D. End of Civilization
      1. conquered by: Spanish
      2. date: 1542

II. Aztec
   A. Background Information
      1. date: 1400's A.D.
      2. location: Mexico
   B. Way of life
      1. Agriculture: chinampas
      2. Religion
         a. gods: Quetzalcoatl, Chicomecoatl
         b. temples: Teotihuacan – Mexico City
   C. Accomplishments: Huitzilopochtli
   D. End of Civilization
      1. conquered by: Cortés
      2. date: 1519

III. Inca
   A. Background Information
      1. date: 1438 to 1532 A.D.
      2. location: Peru and Chile
   B. Way of life
      1. Agriculture: terracing/irrigation
      2. Religion
         a. gods: Inti – the sun
         b. temples: Machu Picchu
   C. Government: empire
   C. Accomplishments
      1. fine stonework
      2. quipo for counting
   D. End of Civilization
      1. conquered by: Pizarro
      2. date: 1532

(Government: empire — fierce warriors — calendar/sunstone — cities)

Page 25

45

A Brave Young Woman

(3) The king wanted to test her to see if she really did possess extraordinary powers. He disguised himself and put one of his noble men on the throne. Joan saw right through the disguise and went immediately to the real king with her request. He tested her again, and she was able to tell him what he prayed to God when he was alone. The king was convinced of her powers.

(4) Joan and her army went to Orleans in April of 1429, and defeated the English in only ten days. Charles had never been officially crowned king because the city of Reims, the coronation site for French kings, was in enemy territory. After the victory at Orleans, Joan escorted Charles to Reims, where he was crowned King on July 17, 1429.

(5) Joan wanted to free France completely from the English, so she went again into battle outside Paris. This time she was wounded and captured by the English. Rather than return her to the French in exchange for ransom, as was the custom, the English kept her as a prisoner.

(6) Like the French, the English also believed Joan had supernatural powers. Where the French king thought they came from God, the English thought they were from the devil. Joan was charged with witchcraft by a French tribunal sympathetic to the English. She was found guilty and burned at the stake on May 30, 1431 in Rouen, France. Her ashes were thrown into the Seine River.

(7) Later, her family requested a new trial, and in 1456, she was found innocent. Although it was too late to save her life, she was declared a saint. Saint Joan of Arc is recognized on the date of her death, May 30.

(1) Imagine a 17 year old girl going to her king and telling him she would like to lead his army to victory. Even more amazing, imagine the king agreeing with her. You may think this is a far-fetched story, but it really happened.

(2) The year was 1429. Joan of Arc was only 17 years old when she went to King Charles VII of France to tell him she had seen a vision and heard the voices of saints. God wanted her to free France from the English. She was to lead the French army against the English of Orleans.

Page 28

Saint Patrick

Read these three paragraphs about Saint Patrick's Day. Each one has a different purpose.

1. Today is a special day. Almost everyone is dressed in green. There are shamrocks everywhere. People are wearing buttons that say, "Kiss me, I'm Irish." Many of the big cities have parades. People are dancing to Irish music as they celebrate Saint Patrick's Day, March 17.

2. Even people who are or are not Irish love to celebrate Saint Patrick's Day, but many don't even know who Saint Patrick was. He was born and lived in England, which was then a part of the great Roman Empire, around 400 A.D. When Patrick was sixteen, pirates captured him and sold him as a slave in Ireland. After several years, he escaped and returned to England. He went to France and studied in a monastery. One night he had a dream telling him to return to Ireland. He returned and built many churches, schools, and monasteries as he taught Irish people about his faith. He also taught people to read and write. He was loved and respected by the Irish people and was made their patron saint. They celebrate his feast day on March 17.

3. On Saint Patrick's Day in the United States, people celebrate with parties and parades. In Ireland, however, it is a religious celebration. The people attend church and celebrate reverently. Patrick is credited with the conversion of the Irish to Christianity.

Write the number of the paragraph beside the sentence that tells the main idea of that paragraph.

3 In Ireland, Saint Patrick's Day is a religious celebration and is observed differently than in the United States.

1 Today is Saint Patrick's Day.

2 Saint Patrick was a bishop who went to Ireland and built many churches. He was loved by the Irish people.

Write your own paragraph about Saint Patrick's Day, in which the main idea tells how you celebrate St. Patrick's Day at your home or school.

Answers will vary.

Page 31

Crazy Maze

A labyrinth is a maze of many confusing passageways. You may have played labyrinth games on a computer, but have you ever been inside a life-sized labyrinth and tried to find your way out?

In Greek mythology, there is a story about King Minos of Crete. He hired an inventor named Daedalus to build a large labyrinth where he imprisoned the Minotaur, a monster with the body of a man and the head of a bull. Each year, King Minos sacrificed seven young men and seven young maidens from Athens to the Minotaur by sending them into the labyrinth.

One year, the son of the king of Athens volunteered to go as a sacrifice. He was determined to kill the Minotaur and find his way out again so no more Athenians would have to be sacrificed. When he arrived on the island of Crete, King Minos' daughter, Ariadne fell in love with this man. She gave him a magic ball of string and told him to tie one end to the beginning of the maze so he could follow it back to find his way out. He did as she instructed and was able to find his way through the maze to kill the Minotaur, to kill him, and to rescue the thirteen others who had also been sacrificed that year.

Pick the correct word or phrase from the word boxes to fill in the blanks to tell the main idea of this story.

| 1. game / maze / computer | 2. Crete / Athens / Rome | 3. Minotaur / Ariadne / Daedalus |
| 4. Daedalus / Minos / Ariadne | 5. daughter / Daedalus / Minotaur | 6. falling in love with Ariadne / following a string / remembering the way |

Another word for a labyrinth is a (1) **maze**. It was built by (3) **Daedalus** for King (4) **Minos** so he could keep the (5) **Minotaur** prisoner there. One young man found his way through the maze. If you go the correct way and pick up each letter you pass, you will find the name of the king's son from Athens **Theseus**.

One of the most famous labyrinths is found in (2) **Crete**.

Page 27

Two Holidays

Each year, the citizens of the United States celebrate two holidays to remember service men and women who fought in wars to preserve citizens' freedom. On November 11, Veterans Day is celebrated, and on May 30, or the last Monday in May, Memorial Day.

November 11, 1918, was the day a treaty was signed between the Germans and the allied forces of the United States, France, Great Britain, Russia, and Italy, putting an end to World War I. This day was first called Armistice Day, but is now called Veterans Day. On that day, George Honey, an Australian journalist, asked that whole world to remain silent for two minutes as the treaty was signed. Even the radios were silent. The Great Silence is still observed in some Australian celebrations.

Memorial Day began after the Civil War, when people began decorating the graves of soldiers who had died in the war. Although many claim to have started the tradition, Congress declared Waterloo, New York, the birthplace of Memorial Day when the whole community held a celebration on May 5, 1866. In 1868, the Grand Army of the Republic declared a ceremony at the National Cemetery in Arlington, Virginia. They called it Decoration Day because they decorated the graves of soldiers. The holiday stuck, but the name was changed to Memorial Day. On this day, many communities hold parades in remembrance of servicemen and women who have given their lives for the freedom of the United States of America.

On the space in front of each of the following key words and phrases, write either V (Veterans Day) or M (Memorial Day) to show the correct holiday.

M May 30	V November 11	V World War I
V Great Silence	M decorated graves	V Waterloo, NY
V George Honey	M Civil War	M Grand Army of the Republic
M Arlington Cemetery	V Armistice Day	M parades
M Decoration Day		V signing of peace treaty

CAPT. NICHOLAS PARKER — LT. MATTHEW SIMMONS

Page 30

Who's My Neighbor?

This is a logic puzzle. Logic puzzles help you develop thinking skills. Label each house with the correct person's name. Use the clues below to help you match each person with the correct house.

Use the grid to help you figure out this puzzle. Put an X in each box that could not possibly work, and an O when you have a definite match. Once you record an O, place an X in all remaining boxes in that row and column. Clue #1 is done for you.

Clues
1. Cody lives in house #4
2. Kris only has one neighbor
3. Kris's neighbor is not Sam
4. Sue's house is yellow
5. Cody and Sam live next to Sue
6. Max's house has one window

	1	2	3	4	5
Max	O	X	X	X	X
Sam	X	O	X	X	X
Kris	X	X	X	X	O
Sue	X	X	O	X	X
Cody	X	X	X	O	X

Houses: Max 1, Sam 2, Sue 3, Cody 4, Kris 5

1. What is the main phrase to look for when organizing the houses? **next to or neighbor**

2. Give the number(s) of any clues that were not helpful. **4**

   Why were they not helpful? **The houses are all black and white. This activity helps develop thinking skills.**

3. What is the main reason for doing this activity? **helps develop thinking skills.**

Page 26

A Brave Young Woman (cont.)

Circle the answer that best tells the main idea of each numbered paragraph.

1. a. Something amazing might happen involving a 17 year old girl and a king
   b. This story is not possible, therefore, it is fiction.
   c. A story about a girl asking her king if she may lead his army is really true

2. a. Joan of Arc led the French army into a battle of Orleans.
   b. Joan was to see the king
   c. Joan heard voices telling her to lead the French in battle

3. a. Joan was a good test taker.
   b. The king tested Joan to see if what she claimed was true.
   c. Joan did not pass the first test, so she had to take another.

4. a. Joan was a military genius who defeated the English.
   b. The king was not officially crowned because the English held Reims.
   c. After defeating the English, Joan led the king to Reims to be officially crowned

5. a. Joan liked wars, so she kept fighting until her capture.
   b. Joan was wounded, captured, and held prisoner by the English.
   c. The French army would not pay a ransom so the English to get Joan back.

6. a. Joan was tried for witchcraft and burned at the stake.
   b. There is a debate about whether Joan's power came from God or the devil.
   c. Joan's ashes were thrown into the Seine River.

7. a. Joan's family wanted to bring her back to life, so they requested a new trial.
   b. Joan was later found innocent and declared to be a saint.
   c. Joan is recognized on the date of her death.

Page 29

Tape Recorders

Did you ever listen to a tape and wonder how music could be produced from that little cassette? Here is how it works:

Each cassette has a **supply reel** which contains a roll of **magnetic tape**. It also has a **take-up reel** to collect the tape after it runs through the recorder. A small motor turns a wheel called the **capstan**. A **pinch roller** pushes the magnetic tape against the capstan which pulls the tape past the **idler** (a wheel which helps control the speed and flow of the tape) and several heads to the take-up reel.

The heads are small electromagnets. The first head is the **erase head**. It produces a strong magnetic field to remove any previous recording. The second head is a **recording head**. A microphone converts sounds to electric currents. As the tape passes the head, which has a small gap, the magnetic field magnetizes iron oxide particles onto the tape in a pattern. The third head is a **play-back head**. The magnetic patterns on the tape generate electric current which is picked up by an amplifier to strengthen the current and then sent on to the speaker to reproduce recorded sounds. The speed at which the tape passes the heads, inches per second, determines the quality of the tape. A faster speed produces a better quality tape.

The main idea of this article is to explain how tape recorders work.

Label the diagram below with each part of the cassette tape as described in the article (supply reel, magnetic tape, take-up reel, capstan, pinch roller, idler, erase head, recording head, and playback head).

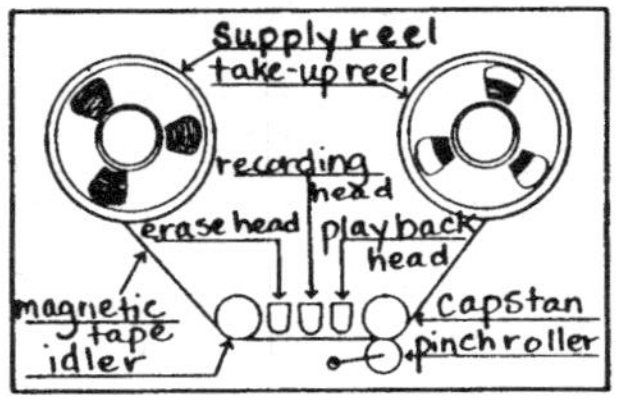

Page 32

Legal and Binding Contract

When lawyers write legal contracts, they often use words that are not part of our everyday vocabulary. Read the contract to understand what is being offered to you and what your part of the bargain is. Each legal word in italics is followed by a more common word or phrase in parentheses.

It is hearby agreed that the *bearer* (owner) of this contract, who shall be named ____________, hereafter named said student, shall be *entitled to* (given) privileges granted herein in accordance with the *contingencies* (rules) listed herein by ____________, hereafter named *grantor* (giver).

Contingencies:

- *Whereas* (if) said student completes all assignments *designated* (assigned) by grantor of this contract, and
- Whereas said student arrives in the classroom at the scheduled and appointed time, and
- Whereas said student *refrains* (keeps) from negative behavior in the classroom, including but not limited to, talking out of turn, *excessive* (over) use of pencil sharpening device, cruel behavior toward other classmates, in addition to any other behavior deemed unacceptable by grantor, then...

If it be *ascertained* (decided) by grantor that said student has successfully met contingencies above, grantor hereby commits to excusing student from one homework assignment without any *due consequences* (penalties).

Contract becomes *valid* (good) upon signatures of both said student and grantor.

Contract must be *redeemed* (traded in) within 30 days of date signed below or contract becomes *null and void* (no good).

Limitations (restrictions): Should said student *expressly* (purposefully) *violate contingencies* (break a rule) during that 30 day period, all *obligations* (promises) on the part of grantor shall *cease* and *terminate* (end).

Bearer signature	Date
Grantor signature	Date
Homework assignment excused	Date redeemed

1. What is the main purpose of the contract? to offer the student an excuse from one homework assignment.
2. What do you have to do to redeem it? Complete work, be on time, be good.
3. What must your teacher do to make it valid? Sign it.
4. When does it expire? 30 days after signed
5. What are its limitations? If a student breaks a rule, it is no longer valid.

Page 33

April Fools' Day

On the first of April we celebrate April Fools' Day. It's a fun day set aside to play jokes and make people laugh. How did it start? There are many theories.

(1) There is a Roman myth from 2000 years ago about the goddess of grain and harvest, Ceres, and her daughter, Proserpina, were out picking flowers one spring day. The god of the dead, Pluto, saw Proserpina and thought her very beautiful. He kidnapped her to bring her to the land of the dead to be his queen. She did not want to go and cried out for help. Ceres heard her and began searching for her, but it was too late. Ceres could not enter the land of the dead. She had been fooled by Pluto. Some say this was the beginning of April fooling.

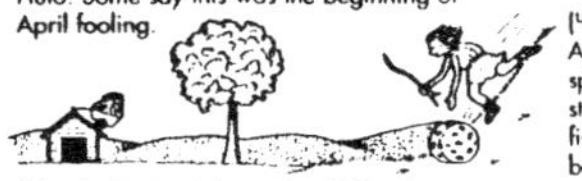

(2) In England during the 1200s, there was a custom that any ground the king walked on become a public road. One day, King John was out for a stroll and wanted to walk through the meadow of Gotham. The people did not want their meadow to become a road, so they locked the gate to keep him out. The king became angry and decided to punish the people of Gotham. He sent an officer to Gotham. The people heard he was coming and joined together in a plan to fool the king. When the officer arrived, he found some people trying to drown a fish in a pond, others putting wagons on top of barns to protect the roofs from the sun, and still others rolling cheese down a hill to market. When the king heard all this, he decided that the people were all such fools that he didn't punish them. Some say that's how April Fools' began.

(3) Until 1564, the New Year began on April 1. King Charles IX of France decided to switch to the Gregorian calendar, which began with January 1 as New Year's Day. Some people either didn't hear about the change or didn't like the change, and they continued to celebrate on April 1. Others began to play jokes on those who still celebrated on April 1. This fooling became a custom in France.

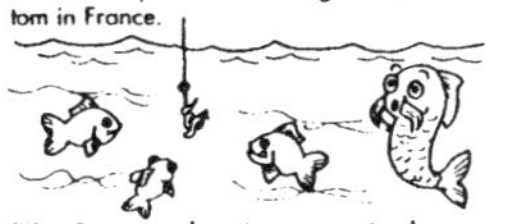

(4) Some say there is a connection between April Fools' Day and catching fish. In the spring when all the young fish hatched, the streams were bursting with fish. These young fish were easily fooled by a hook and could be caught with little effort. French people who were easily fooled were called "poisson d'Avril," or April Fish. Even Napoleon Bonaparte was called "poisson d'Avril" for marrying his second wife on April 1.

(5) In the 1700s, in Scotland, there was a tradition on April 1 called "hunting the gowk" (a cuckoo bird). Someone was chosen to deliver a message quite a distance away. Unbeknownst to the deliverer, the message read, "April 1, Hunt the gowk another mile." So when the message was read, the deliverer was sent on yet another errand. When he finally returned, having accomplished nothing, he'd find everyone laughing.

We don't know for sure exactly where or how April Fools' Day started, but it continues to be a fun day for pranksters in many countries around the world.

Page 34

April Fools' Day (cont.)

In each of the following, circle the letter of the sentence that best describes the main idea of each numbered paragraph. There are many statements that are true, but only one will answer the question asked.

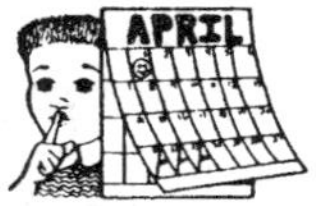

What is the main idea of this reading?

a. The tradition of April Fools' Day was started in France.
(b.) There are several stories about how April Fools' Day started.
c. It is fun to play jokes on April Fools' Day.

1. (a.) Pluto may have played the first April Fools' Day trick by kidnapping Proserpina from Ceres.
   b. Ceres was the goddess of grain and harvest, and Pluto was the god of death.
   c. Proserpina was kidnapped and made queen of the land of the dead.
2. a. King John liked to walk and got angry when he couldn't walk where he wanted.
   b. The people of Gotham were very foolish, and so they were called the first April fools.
   (c.) April Fools' Day may have started when the people of Gotham fooled the king to avoid punishment.
3. a. The date of New Year's Day was changed from April 1 to January 1 in 1564.
   (b.) The king changed New Year's Day to January 1, and tricks were played on the people who still celebrated it on April 1.
   c. April Fools' Day used to be celebrated on January 1, instead of April 1.
4. (a.) There may be a connection between April fish and April Fools' Day, because the spring fish were easily fooled, as are people on April Fools' Day.
   b. In the spring, fish are easy to catch because there are so many of them.
   c. Napoleon Bonaparte was one of the first April fools because he got married on April 1.
5. a. The people in Scotland hunted a bird called a gowk, or cuckoo bird, for the first time each year on April 1.
   b. When someone read a message that said, "April 1, Hunt the gowk another mile," they made the person who delivered the note run.
   (c.) A traditional joke played on April Fools' Day in Scotland was to have someone run an errand called "hunting the gowk," in which the person is sent on errand after errand and never accomplishes anything.

Page 35

Bill of Rights

When the founding fathers of the United States wrote the Constitution, they added ten amendments, called the Bill of Rights, to be sure certain rights would never be taken from the American people. Since that time, more amendments have been added. Here is the original Bill of Rights, as taken from the National Archives and Records Administration.

Amendment 1. Congress shall make no law respecting an establishment of religion, or prohibiting the free exercise thereof; or abridging the freedom of speech, or of the press; or the right of the people peaceably to assemble, and to petition the Government for a redress of grievances.

Amendment 2. A well regulated Militia, being necessary to the security of a free State, the right of the people to keep and bear Arms, shall not be infringed.

Amendment 3. No Soldier shall, in time of peace be quartered in any house, without the consent of the Owner, nor in time of war, but in a manner to be prescribed by law.

Amendment 4. The right of the people to be secure in their persons, houses, papers, and effects, against unreasonable searches and seizures, shall not be violated, and no Warrants shall issue, but upon probable cause, supported by Oath or affirmation, and particularly describing the place to be searched, and the persons or things to be seized.

Amendment 5. No person shall be held to answer for a capital, or otherwise infamous crime, unless on a presentment or indictment of a Grand Jury, except in cases arising in the land or naval forces, or in the Militia, when in actual service in time of War or public danger; nor shall any person be subject for the same offence to be twice put in jeopardy of life or limb; nor shall be compelled in any criminal case to be a witness against himself, nor be deprived of life, liberty, or property, without due process of law; nor shall private property be taken for public use, without just compensation.

Amendment 6. In all criminal prosecutions, the accused shall enjoy the right to a speedy and public trial, by an impartial jury of the State and district wherein the crime shall have been committed, which district shall have been previously ascertained by law, and to be informed of the nature and cause of the accusation; to be confronted with the witnesses against him; to have compulsory process for obtaining witnesses in his favor, and to have the Assistance of Counsel for his defence.

Amendment 7. In suits at common law, where the value in controversy shall exceed twenty dollars, the right of trial by jury shall be preserved, and no fact tried by a jury, shall be otherwise reexamined in any Court of the United States, than according to the rules of the common law.

Amendment 8. Excessive bail shall not be required, nor excessive fines imposed, nor cruel and unusual punishments inflicted.

Amendment 9. The enumeration in the Constitution, of certain rights, shall not be construed to deny or disparage others retained by the people

Amendment 10. The powers not delegated to the United States by the Constitution, nor prohibited by it to the States, are reserved to the States respectively, or to the people.

Page 36

Bill of Rights (cont.)

Match each amendment in the Bill of Rights to the picture and caption that best tells the main idea of each by writing the number of the amendment on the line next to the caption.

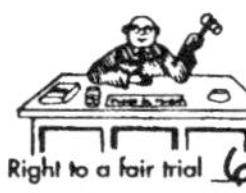

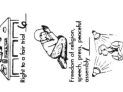

Right to a fair trial 6

Right to keep and bear arms 2

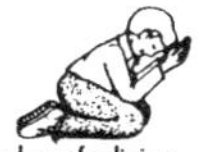

Freedom of religion, speech, press, peaceful assembly 1

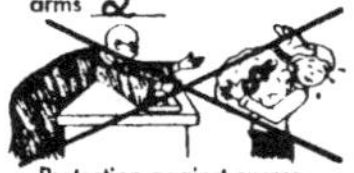

Protection against excessive bails, fines, and punishments 8

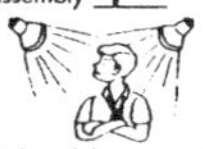

Rights of the accused 5

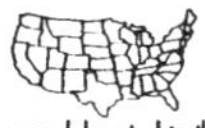

Powers delegated to the states 10

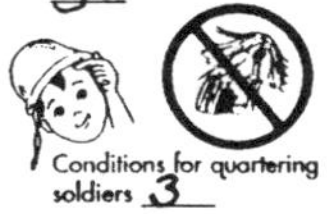

Conditions for quartering soldiers 3

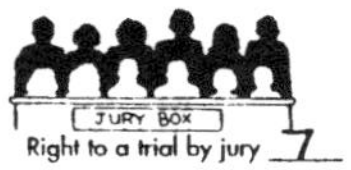

Right to a trial by jury 7

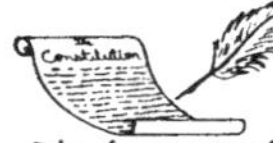

Rules of construction of the constitution 9

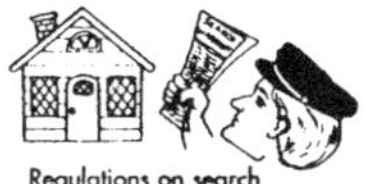

Regulations on search and seizure 4

Page 37

Let's Chat!

We live in a very mobile society, which means that friends and family are often moving away from each other. Fortunately, modern technology has made it easy to keep in touch. You no longer have to wait weeks for letters to travel back and forth, nor pay expensive phone bills. With Internet Relay Chat (IRC), you can communicate with people almost anywhere in the world for the cost of a local phone call to your Internet server. You can "chat" with each other by typing messages on your keyboard. Since typing takes a lot longer than talking, people who often use IRC have developed abbreviations which are commonly used and understood to help speed things up. Here are some of them:

BCNU—Be seeing you!	BTW—By the way
CUL8R—See you later	IMO—In my opinion
GMTA—Great minds think alike	J/K—Just kidding
LTNO—Long time no see	NP—No problem
ROFL—Rolling on the floor laughing	THX—Thanks
RUOK—Are you OK?	TTFN—Ta ta for now
WTG—Way to Go!	WYSIWYG—What you see is what you get!

Abbreviations are made up by shortening words like this: CN U RD THS (Can you read this)?

In a conversation, the tone of a person's voice or the expression on their face help you to better understand their meaning. On the Internet, you cannot see a face or hear a voice, but you can add emotional expression to your messages by using "emoticons" (emotional icons). These are made by combining various symbols such as a colon, hyphen, and parenthesis to make a smiley face :). You may have to turn it sideways to recognize it. Here are some others:

:)	very happy	:O	yawn
:* or :-*	kiss	@	screaming
:(	crying	:D	laughing out loud
%)	confused	:((	very sad
;)	winking	>:(	angry
:/	sad	:/	undecided

Page 40

A Few of My Favorite Things (cont.)

1. What was the main reason for conducting this survey? **To see if there is a difference in the preferences of boys and girls.**

2. What was the favorite in each category?

	boys	girls	combined
Sport	Soccer	basketball	soccer
Subject	foreign language	social studies	foreign language

3. What was the least favorite in each category?

	boys	girls	combined
Sport	tennis	football	tennis
Subject	language arts	math	language arts

4. In which areas was there a significant difference between the boys' and the girls' favorite things? (significant means more than 2 or 3 out of 100) **football, baseball, soccer, math, music, science, social studies, foreign language**

5. Did the survey accomplish what it set out to do? **Yes**

6. What are your favorites? Sport **Answers will vary.**

Page 39

A Few of My Favorite Things

A survey was taken of a group of 200 fifth- and sixth- grade students, 100 girls and 100 boys. They were asked about their favorite things to see if there was a difference between the preferences of boys and girls. The graphs below show the results.

Boys   Girls   Combined

Favorite Sport to Play
Football, Baseball, Basketball, Soccer, Volleyball, Tennis
0 10 20 30 40 50 60 70 80

Favorite School Subject
Math, Music, Science, Social Studies, Language Arts, Foreign Language
0 10 20 30 40 50 60 70 80

Page 38

Let's Chat! (cont.)

Circle the letter of the best answer.

1. The main idea of this article is to...
   a. tell you how to use the Internet.
   b. introduce Internet Relay Chat.
   c. teach you a new language.

2. Users of IRC use abbreviations...
   a. to have their own private language that no one else can understand.
   b. to be able to communicate faster while typing.
   c. because they don't know how to spell words correctly.

3. Emoticons on IRC...
   a. are impossible to show, because it's all typed words.
   b. are not necessary, since you can type words to mean exactly what you want to say.
   c. can be shown using emoticons such as the smiley face.

Here is a chat message to you. Can you read it?
IMO it's TM 4 U 2 HV SM FN with IRC.
SND a message 2 a FRND & HV HM RSPND. TTFN :))

Send your message here.

To:
From: **Answers will vary.**

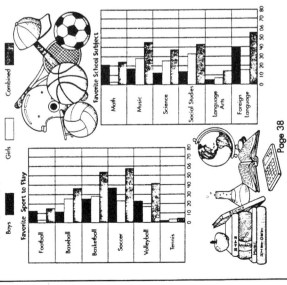

Page 41